What p...

This is a breathtaking tool that will help mothers toward ... ... nancy loss. Liz Mannegren writes with honesty, poignancy, and vulnerability. Not only is she transparent about her own experiences, but she guides readers in unpacking their own grief, creating a safe space to write their own stories. This book is a powerful guided journey of faith, hope, and healing.

—Stefanie Tong
Author of *Chasing Light*

Pregnancy loss is a devastating experience that can leave women feeling hopeless. In *Embrace: Clinging to Christ through the Pain of Pregnancy Loss*, Liz Mannegren demonstrates how sharing personal stories and biblical truth give hope to a bereaved mother's hurting heart. Her words both validate grief and place value on the life that was lost. A must-read for any mother who has felt buried by the weight of pregnancy loss.

—Jenny Albers
Blogger at *A Beautifully Burdened Life*

Liz Mannegren has sought to minister to grieving mothers in a way that is incredibly rare. She walks with you through the deep pain of loss while at the same time applying the eternal hope of the gospel to those wounds. I hope many mothers are encouraged to draw nearer still to their Saviour through this wonderful resource.

—Lexi Zuo
Loss Mom

Even though pain and grief are not one-size-fits-all, they are a universal part of human existence. When we're willing to truly hear each other's stories without feeling like we need to say "I know exactly how you feel," we find our own grief softened, and from that comfort we comfort others. Liz Mannegren beautifully tells these stories in a way that brings hope even through heartache and honours the memories of those who are missed.

—Trisha Aristizabal
Pastor

Liz Mannegren's compassionately-written book, *Embrace*, is a soothing balm to the soul of every Momma who has experienced the devastating loss of a pregnancy. With grace and welcoming arms, she and her beautiful contributors share their stories of heartache, grief, survival, and ultimately redemption as they each travel their grief journeys. As readers, we feel a strong connection to them and the hope that comes with knowing we're not walking this path alone.

Each chapter builds solidly upon the previous one and strengthens our resolve to find our peace and acceptance through our bond with Christ. The brilliant journaling prompts that follow enable us to delve into our experiences and come away with newly acquired enlightenment.

Liz Mannegren, through her own story of loss, has gifted us with a treasured book of blessings.

—Lisa Leshaw
Author of *How Are You Feeling, Momma?*

Embrace is a beautiful read. Throughout the pages of this book, Liz Mannegren shares her own infant-loss journey, points readers to the hope they have in Christ, and provides journaling prompts to encourage mothers to write about their loss. A must-read for anyone dealing with the incredible pain of losing their baby.

—Kendra Plett
Labour & Delivery Nurse

With tears rolling down my cheeks, I read this book and felt so loved, understood, and validated in the broken emotions I experienced grieving the child we lost to miscarriage. Whether you lost your child at four weeks or to a stillbirth, whether you lost your child twenty years ago or yesterday, you'll feel comforted to know that the way you're grieving is acceptable. This book is covered in truths from Jesus to help grow your spiritual faith and feel God's presence as you deal with painful memories hidden in your heart.

—Kaleigh Christensen
Blogger at *Messy Footprints*

As a loss mom who has recently walked through three miscarriages of my own, I found this book to be a key tool in helping me understand how to process grief through its different stages and with different people. Liz Mannegren's transparency and heart will touch many lives and give women a place to start after loss. As a birth and bereavement doula, I will be adding this book to my doula bag and recommending it to the families I support through their grief.

—Ashleigh Beaver
Birth and Bereavement Doula

Embrace

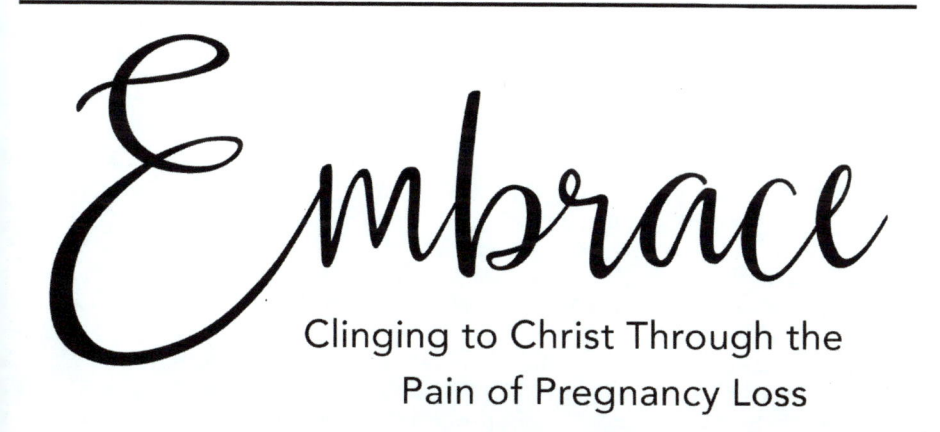

Clinging to Christ Through the Pain of Pregnancy Loss

LIZ MANNEGREN

EMBRACE
Copyright © 2019 by Liz Mannegren

All rights reserved. Neither this publication nor any part of this publication may be reproduced or transmitted in any form or by any means, electronic or mechanical, including photocopying, recording or any information storage and retrieval system, without permission in writing from the author.

Unless otherwise indicated, scripture quotations are taken from The Holy Bible, English Standard Version® (ESV®), copyright © 2001 by Crossway, a publishing ministry of Good News Publishers. Used by permission. All rights reserved. Scripture quotations marked (NIV) are taken from the Holy Bible, NEW INTERNATIONAL VERSION®, NIV® Copyright © 1973, 1978, 1984, 2011 by Biblica, Inc.® Used by permission. All rights reserved worldwide. Scripture quotations marked (NLT) are taken from the Holy Bible, New Living Translation, copyright ©1996, 2004, 2007 by Tyndale House Foundation. Used by permission of Tyndale House Publishers, Inc., Carol Stream, Illinois 60188. All rights reserved. Scripture quotations attributed to the King James Version of the Bible are taken from the Holy Bible, King James Version, which is in the public domain.

Printed in Canada

Print ISBN: 978-1-4866-1928-3
eBook ISBN: 978-1-4866-1929-0

Word Alive Press
119 De Baets Street, Winnipeg, MB R2J 3R9
www.wordalivepress.ca

WORD ALIVE
—PRESS—

FSC
www.fsc.org
MIX
Paper from
responsible sources
FSC® C016245

Cataloguing in Publication may be obtained through Library and Archives Canada

*To Landon, Kära, Björn, Ebba, and Avonlea,
and to all the other babies carried in hearts and loved from afar.*

Contents

1. A Good Place to Start — 1
2. Nobody Said So — 16
3. The Right to Grieve — 27
4. Playing the Blame Game — 40
5. Dealing with Triggers — 55
6. Comparing — 65
7. Supporting a Grieving Spouse — 74
8. Supporting Grieving Children — 88
9. When Words Hurt — 97
10. Holidays and Milestones — 107
11. Finding Ways to Remember — 117
12. Feeling Alone — 129
13. Gratefulness in Support — 140
14. You're Still a Mom — 149
15. Leaning into Grief — 161
16. This Is Not the End — 170

Acknowledgements — 175

Chapter One

A Good Place to Start

I *hate* that you're reading this book.

I know that the only reason you've even picked it up off the shelf is because you or someone you love has been devastated by the loss of a beautiful child. You may be in the process of miscarrying your first baby, or you may have been broken over and over again by the pain of multiple losses. It may be years since you held your stillborn babe in your arms, or you may have just received devastating news at yesterday's ultrasound. Regardless of where you are in this journey, the fact that you're holding this book in your hand tells me that you're looking for a way to better understand and process your grief. This desire is a very good place to start.

With the loss of your precious baby, you've been sadly inaugurated into a community of broken and grieving mothers. This tribe of heartache and blood is not a club that anyone willingly or readily joins, yet it's near bursting at the seams. Across North America, one in six of every *known* pregnancy ends in miscarriage[1], while one in two hundred pregnancies ends in stillbirth.[2] You never thought that it would happen to you, but on that day, as you lay bleeding in the hospital bed with empty arms and a broken heart, you became the unlucky "one."

But the truth is that you are more than just a number on a page. You are more than just a statistic. You are the mother of a beautiful and beloved child whom you will carry in your heart for the rest of your days. Your arms

---

1 "Miscarriage," HealthLink BC, accessed August 15, 2019, https://www.healthlinkbc.ca/health-topics/hw44090#hw44092

2 "Stillbirth," HealthLink BC, accessed August 15, 2019, https://www.healthlinkbc.ca/health-topics/uf9702#uf9703

may be empty, but the crevices of your broken heart have filled with a never-fading love.

In this club of wounded mothers, there's strength to be drawn from our shared heartbreak. There's communion to be found around this table of loss and hope to be seen amidst our individual stories of heartache. Like Amy, who experienced a chemical pregnancy[3] at five weeks; Kristy, who experienced a full-term stillbirth; or Joy, who has mourned six miscarriages and a second-trimester loss, we all have a unique story to share.

This book won't give you answers to that elusive, unanswerable question, "Why?" But I pray that as you turn these pages, you'll find yourself drawn ever closer to the God who knit you together in your own mother's womb. That though the storm rages around you, you will find the place where you can come wobbly-kneed and empty-handed before the throne and whisper, "Even so, it is well with my soul."

But how do we do that? What do we do with this sudden deluge of pain? What does it mean to *embrace* our grief rather than simply run from it?

Throughout this book, we'll look at some of the different facets of life after pregnancy loss. In addition to the stories and experiences shared by other women, each chapter will also conclude with a set of journal prompts that I pray will allow you to dive deeper into your grief and subsequently into Christ.

I know that journal prompts aren't for all us of. (And truthfully, I'm talking to myself here!) I'm the type of person who rarely completes journal questions out of books—especially when it comes to a topic as personal and raw as grief. Journaling for me needs to be a free-flowing and natural response to the aches and depths of my heart. Answering questions makes me feel like I'm back in high school, scribbling trite responses to achieve a good grade. But this process is not about finding the *right* answers. It's about giving space to find truth amidst the cloudiness and uncertainty of grief.

Whether you use the prompts as a jumping off place or dedicatedly work your way through each question one at a time, I'm asking you to at

---

[3] A chemical pregnancy is a pregnancy that has been confirmed by the HCG hormone (via pregnancy test or bloodwork) but is miscarried before an ultrasound can detect the fetus. (This is usually up until the fifth week of pregnancy.) Despite connotations of the word "chemical," it is still very much a real pregnancy and loss.

least *consider* journaling your way through this loss. With an experience as new and overwhelming as this, we may struggle to know where to start. We may not know what questions to ask or what bits of our pain to probe. Journaling is one of many coping methods that can be particularly useful for reflecting and processing. For some, myself included, putting thoughts to paper can be easier than voicing them aloud. As the words spill out of our pens and dance their way across ivory-toned paper, journaling can help us explore our deepest feelings in a safe environment. When we write, we release pent up emotions and learn to better refine or clarify our thoughts. And while the allure of a new, leather-bound notebook might not call out to you in the way it does to me, remember that you don't have to be an eloquent writer to journal. You don't need proper grammar or neat printing. All you need is a blank book, some scrap paper, or your computer.

Fellow loss mom Sarah is just one of many women who will vouch for the healing that can come through writing. Being married for little over a year, Sarah and her husband were excited when they quickly became pregnant. With a September due date circled on their calendar, the couple headed in for a twenty-week ultrasound, only to be devastated by the news that there was no heartbeat. Their son, Brett, was born at the end of April, still and tiny and silent. Six months later, they started trying again and were heartbroken once more by a Thanksgiving Day miscarriage: a little girl whom they named Maggie.

Sarah says, "One of the biggest things in helping me to process my grief was writing about it. I needed to write down my thoughts and feelings in a way that was clear enough that when I hit publish on a blog post, others would understand me. This made me process my grief differently than before I started writing. When it's a jumble in your head, it's hard to work through all the emotions. When you give your thoughts direction, it brings clarity."

For many of us, it's easy to bottle up our grief, store it away, and say that we'll deal with it another day. Sometimes our answers to the difficult questions hurt too much or they feel embarrassing or shameful. But journaling isn't about finding "the right answers." It's about being honest with yourself. Dulci, a mother of four precious babies, one stillborn at twenty-one weeks, says, "Writing and sharing my story is how I process my grief in a healthy way. If it stays all in my head and heart, it festers."

Like Sarah and Dulci, I too experienced loss, and along the way I discovered the strength that can come through journaling. As emotions spilled out of my pen, I uncovered feelings that had been hidden deep within my bruised and broken heart. Working through my grief taught me more about myself and my relationship with God, and through this long, still-unravelling process, I discovered hope. As I leaned into my grief, I began to discover the woman that God was moulding and shaping to look more like Him. I began to catch tiny glimpses of the Father's heart for the broken, and I was reminded of what it looks like to truly live without fear of tomorrow.

There's no denying that grief hurts and that this loss will forever be a defining part of your life. The sharp edges will fade with time, but this sliver of grief remains. That's why this book is not about finding complete healing or getting everything back to "the way it was before." This book doesn't aim to "fix" things or tell you how to feel. This book is simply about embracing your grief and bringing light to the truth of your story. It's about leaning into our grief and allowing Christ to redeem and restore what has been broken and destroyed.

Sometimes one of the easiest places to begin in our journaling is with our child's story. Whether you spent one day or nine months together, their little life was precious and valuable and worth exploring. Your story may not look like mine. It may not look like Sarah's or Joy's or any of the other women in this book. Our pain is each our own. But as we work our way through these occasionally tear-stained pages, I pray that you will discover strength and joy in the messy but oh-so-beautiful story that *you've* been given. I pray that you will find *hope*.

I was twenty-two years old when I lost my first child. It was my first pregnancy, and I was filled with the naïve optimism of one who had not yet experienced loss. Never dreaming of anything except a happily-ever-after ending, I waddled in and out of doctor's appointments as if untouchable. I didn't know that stillbirths still occurred in North America, and while miscarriages may happen to other people, they certainly wouldn't happen to me.

I was young and healthy, and there were no warning signs or family history of loss. I diligently popped prenatal vitamins and actively avoided all pregnancy dangers. I said good-bye to sushi and deli meats, hot tubs and rollercoasters, and hello to light exercise, leafy greens, and afternoon naps. By all accounts, I was doing *everything right*. And yet one summer evening, seven months into a beautiful pregnancy, I was forced to say good-bye to my firstborn.

This is my story. It's full of cracks and imperfections, and heartache after heartache. But as you read through the next few pages, I hope you see the echo of Christ's deep, redeeming love throughout our darkest of days. I pray that our story and the stories of women throughout this book will allow you to begin reflecting on God's faithfulness throughout your own loss. I pray that you will find comfort in shared grief and in the knowledge that *you are not alone in your pain.*

"I'm pregnant."

Clutching the pink-striped pregnancy test, I waved it anxiously in front of my husband's confused face. "I'm pregnant," I repeated again for clarity, struggling to shake off the shock of this unexpected discovery.

We'd been married for over half a year and were just settling into life together as a couple. Diapers and late-night feeds weren't supposed to be included in our newly wedded bliss. Gone were the dreams of worldwide travels, spontaneous date nights, and the house with the white picket fence. We hadn't counted on life as three, yet here I was barely into my twenties, six weeks pregnant, and feeling nauseous.

I spent the next two weeks fighting down the sense of panic that gurgled alongside my churning stomach. Worrying and wondering about what the future held, I felt overwhelmed by the prospect of motherhood. I was not yet able to comprehend the great gift I was carrying, and had no inkling of the radical shaking my world was about to face.

At exactly eight weeks into my pregnancy, I arrived at the ultrasound clinic with a bursting bladder and a nervous gut. With grainy photos flashing just out of sight, I lay on the narrow table and waited for the technician to slowly and methodically finish her exam. Giving a little smile, she turned her computer screen towards me and awaited my reaction.

Pressed up against the grey ultrasound photo were two beautiful blobs of genetics. The words "Baby A" and "Baby B" sat smack in the middle of the screen, and I couldn't tear my eyes away. My heart felt like butter melting on hot popcorn. My smile stretched wide across my face, cracking my lips and hurting my cheeks with its intensity. We were pregnant with twins! As overwhelmed as I'd been feeling moments earlier, this news should have given me an even greater abundance of anxiety. And yet lying there in a blue hospital gown with ultrasound goop oozing across my belly, I felt nothing but peace. My fears dissipated and my heart beat with the familiar, all-encompassing reassurance that everything was going to be okay. With a fistful of black and white photos in my pocket, I left the clinic feeling ready to take on the world. I'd walked into the ultrasound as an individual, but I walked out as a mother.

Feeling as if I was drenched in "pregnancy glow," the rest of the first trimester passed without major complaint. Arriving at the obstetrician's office at ten weeks along, our jaws hit the floor once more as we discovered that we were pregnant with *identical* twins.

Any pregnancy involving multiples is considered "high risk." Since our type of identical twins shared a placenta, that risk was raised even higher. Still, I remained unfazed. I may have been labelled high risk, but I certainly didn't feel it. Over and over again, doctors and hospital staff told us that we were a "casebook-perfect twin pregnancy." Their reassurance glided over us like silk and masked any nerves.

Every two weeks we made our way to the hospital for another ultrasound. We joyfully waited as technicians carefully measured and analyzed the growth of our beautiful boys. Each photo felt like an opportunity for my husband and me to bond with them further, and the love we felt for them grew stronger with each passing day.

After the gender reveal at twenty-weeks, we began calling our boys by name: Alistair and Landon, and quickly learned their personalities. Alistair was steady, calm, and dependable, while Landon whirled and somersaulted his way across my belly, earning him the nickname "monkey."

When we weren't at ultrasounds or doctors' appointments, I worked as an administrative assistant at my local church. My feet had swelled alongside my stomach, and I was thankful for a job that allowed me to spend my days seated around an office desk. As I answered emails and printed bulletins, I often sang along to praise songs on the radio. The boys seemed to enjoy these quiet moments of worship as much as I did. I would spend hours amazed at the endless ripples that danced across my belly as I whispered and sang along to the music.

It was during one of these days that I stumbled across the old hymn, "Nearer My God to Thee" by Sarah Adams. Probably most commonly known as the song that was played while the *Titanic* sunk, its beautiful melody and heartfelt words seemed to catch and stir someplace deep within me.

Nearer, my God, to thee, nearer to thee!
E'en though it be a cross that raiseth me,
Still all my song shall be,
Nearer, my God, to thee;
Nearer, my God, to thee, nearer to thee![4]

The song played on endless repeat throughout the day, and I was often moved to tears listening to it. Very quickly, these words became a prayer over my pregnancy: that while my boys were still in my womb, they would know God, and that for the rest of their lives they would be ever drawing nearer to Him. Little did I know how significant that prayer would become.

A week after my decision to take early maternity leave, I began to notice a reduction in fetal movement. Quickly whipping out my all-knowing smartphone, I forced my fears aside and decided to trust Google instead. I took comfort in pregnancy forums and mom bloggers who said that "at thirty-one weeks, twin moms may begin feeling reduced movement, as space in the womb is cramped." For the next twenty-four hours, I tried to convince myself that this was the case. In all likelihood, the boys *were* cramped in there. I didn't want to waste everyone's time by making a needless hospital trip. We'd had an ultrasound three days earlier, and everything

---

[4] Sarah F. Adams, "Nearer, My God, To Thee," verse 1, 1841, http://www.hymntime.com/tch/pdf/n/e/a/Nearer,%20My%20God,%20to%20Thee.pdf.

had been perfect. What could change so drastically in less than a week? While I knew in my heart that something wasn't quite right, I didn't want to believe it.

When my husband arrived home from work to find me in a puddle of tears on the floor, he finally convinced me to take a quick trip to the hospital. We had called ahead and the doctor's only question was, "How soon can you get here?"

Arriving at the labour and delivery unit, we had barely gotten seated in the plastic waiting room chair before the nurse called us in. As I stood to follow her, my t-shirt bounced with the impact of a huge, stomach-stretching kick from Landon. Besides hiccups and little flutters, this was the first belly-morphing kick I'd felt in two days.

"Great," I muttered to myself, "we've come here for nothing. Of course, *now* the boys have decided to wake up and stretch!"

I didn't know that that was the last time I'd ever feel my son move. How could I have guessed that this was his only way of saying good-bye? How could I have heard the words that this farewell kick carried? With his last bit of strength, Landon told me, "Mommy, I love you but it's time for me to go home. Don't worry about me. I'm going to be okay now."

My tears flow freely as I write this. I didn't remember this moment until days later, but it will *always* be one of my most treasured memories.

While in my womb, Landon and Alistair had developed "acute twin-to-twin transfusion," a syndrome that only occurs with identical twins. When we arrived at the hospital, the boys' heart rates were dangerously low, but they were both still alive. It was clear to the medical staff, however, that they needed to act quickly. Less than fifteen minutes after we'd pulled into the hospital parking lot, my bed was being rushed down the hallway towards the operating room; my husband was left stunned and alone in the hallway outside.

As I lay on the narrow operating table, I felt scared and vulnerable. The anesthesiologist pressed a plastic mask tight against my face, and I gave out one last strangled prayer, "Lord, I lay the three of us in your hands." It was then that my world went black.

Though like the wanderer, the sun gone down,
Darkness be over me, my rest a stone;
Yet in my dreams I'd be, nearer my God, to Thee.
Nearer, my God, to Thee, nearer to Thee.

There let the way appear, steps unto Heav'n;
All that Thou sendest me, in mercy giv'n;
Angels to beckon me nearer, my God, to Thee.
Nearer, my God, to Thee, nearer to Thee.[5]

Over an hour later, I groggily tried to awaken myself from the fog of anesthesia. My tongue felt thick as I tried to slur the word, "twins?" at the nurse seated beside me. She stood up and silently ushered my husband into the room. He appeared at the foot of my bed, shaky and devastated, crying out with the weight of his grief. "Liz, we lost Landon."

Four words: that was all it took for my hopes and dreams to shatter.

They wrapped my son's tiny body in a pale green hospital towel and laid him in my arms, my tears sprinkling his still warm cheeks. I held him until he grew cold, until I knew that this wasn't just some horrible, terrible nightmare. I held him until I knew that he wasn't coming back.

Our second-born son was in the NICU, ventilated and struggling for life, but alive. I felt overwhelmed. I had been jerked from my blissful, "perfect" pregnancy into an alternate reality. Suddenly, I found myself fighting to deal with the contradictions found in my deepest grief and my greatest joy, a birthday and a death date all wrapped into one: the stories of my two beautiful boys.

That night, I lay awake staring at the ceiling tiles, tossing and turning until rays of sunlight began peeking through the slats of the hospital blinds. In less than twelve hours, my life had broken, and I didn't know how I could ever put it back together again.

My husband crawled onto the uncomfortable hospital bed beside me and we clung to one another. We were both emotionally numb and physically exhausted. Wailing and praying, we huddled over the starched sheets

---

5   Adams, "Nearer, My God, to Thee," verses 2 and 3.

and sobbed, the sound of our tears echoing throughout the maternity ward around us. Turning up the volume on my husband's iPhone, we began to listen to the song that had been so important to me throughout my entire pregnancy: "Nearer my God to Thee."

> *Or, if on joyful wing cleaving the sky,*
> *Sun, moon, and stars forgot, upward I'll fly,*
> *Still all my song shall be, nearer, my God, to Thee.*
> *Nearer, my God, to Thee, nearer to Thee.*[6]

The music swelled out of the little speaker, filling the room and breaking my heart all over again. In anguish, I cried out, "God! I know that I prayed this prayer throughout my entire pregnancy, but when I asked for my boys to be nearer to you, I didn't ask you to take them away from me!"

There was no audible reply, but what we received was just as refreshing. In the midst of my deepest sorrow, that stuffy hospital room began to fill with the most incredible sense of peace. I knew that God had not abandoned us; this gift He had given was not in vain. Even if I could never see His plan or His purpose for this moment, I knew that He was not finished with our family. The pregnancy had ended, but the story did not.

I had been gifted a glorious seven months of kicks and ultrasounds, whispered prayers, and tiny tickles. I had thirty-one breathtakingly beautiful weeks with my twins, and I wouldn't have traded those moments for anything. Given the opportunity, even knowing the end result, I would gladly have done it all over again for those two precious boys. Using this loss as a reminder of life's fragility, I was determined to savour each and every moment that I was given with my children.

Two years later, we decided to try for another baby and quickly became pregnant. I was overjoyed with the prospect of new life and a pregnancy untainted by such deep sorrow. I fought against the insecurities that arise in a pregnancy after a loss and struggled to bond with the new baby. I hoped that things would change after the first ultrasound, just as they had during my twin pregnancy.

---

6   Adams, "Nearer, My God, to Thee," verse 5.

But we never made it to the ultrasound. We lost that baby at exactly eight weeks, and once again, I began the difficult process of learning to say good-bye to someone you've never met. We strongly felt that this child was a girl and didn't want to leave her nameless. My husband is a proud Swede, so in honour of her Scandinavian roots, we named the baby Kära. (This comes from a Swedish phrase "min kära," meaning "my dear.")

The doctors assured us that this loss wouldn't affect future pregnancies and that "the odds of having two miscarriages in a row are *extremely low*." I was eager to start trying again and anxiously awaited our family's growth. Surely this was enough loss now. Surely next time I'd get to take a baby home.

Three months later we were pregnant again. This time I made it to the ultrasound only to discover that the sac was empty: no heartbeat, no baby. They called it a blighted ovum and told me to wait to miscarry. I awoke each morning wondering if it was the end of another pregnancy. I desperately clung to the hope that the doctors were somehow wrong, but logic told me otherwise.

Two weeks later I said my third heart-ripping farewell. We named him "Björn" (Swedish, meaning "bear"), and I began to wonder if my heart could hold any more.

It wasn't long before it became apparent that my heart *could* hold more—much more. We miscarried Ebba three months later, another eight-week pregnancy that disappeared in the blink of an eye. Four months after that, we said good-bye to our earliest gestational loss: Avonlea. The chemical pregnancy dissolved at just five weeks. Having known about her for a mere seven days, my heart ached and body bled in a different way, but she was no less important than the others. She was no less loved.

> *There in my Father's home, safe and at rest,*
> *There in my Savior's love, perfectly blest;*
> *Age after age to be nearer, my God, to Thee.*
> *Nearer, my God, to Thee, nearer to Thee.*[7]

---

7 Adams, "Nearer, My God, to Thee," verse 6.

I am a mother who has felt the searing pain of loss, a mother who now knows that there is no "safe zone" in pregnancy. I have buried one son and have watched my body slowly reject the lives of four others. I am a mother who has learned that strength can be found in tears and that, despite the pain, there is beauty here too. A year and a half after that last miscarriage, we finally got to bring a baby home from the hospital—our daughter, Adelaide. But while you may only see two, I am the mother of seven.

My story doesn't read the way I'd originally imagined it would. The words in this chapter weave a different tale from the one I'd planned on telling. But this story is mine. This story, with its jagged edges and soggy, tear-stained pages, is *my beautiful love story:* a story of hope, restoration, and the faithfulness of a steadfast God.

As we begin journaling our way through grief, telling our stories seems to be a natural place to begin; but just because it's a good place to start doesn't mean that it will be easy. I know that this isn't the story that you wanted. We'd much rather hold a baby in our arms than a journal damp with tears. But this story deserves to be told, because it belongs to *you.*

Find some quiet time and begin reflecting on and writing out your story. Don't worry about fancy editing or words that you think people want to hear. Be honest with yourself and write whatever comes to mind. Take a deep breath and let it all out. You may fill an entire book with your memories, tears, and little details that you don't want to forget. Or you may feel that your story's joys and sorrows are better captured in a few paragraphs. You may choose to keep your thoughts private, or you may feel led to share them. What you do with this journal is up to you. There's no right or wrong way to journal. The important thing to see is that *you have a story*: a story of a mother who loved so hard it hurt, who fought for her child, and who will never forget her little ones. No one may ever read the words you write, but I pray that as you watch your story unfold on the page in front of you, you will see strength and an inner resilience that you didn't know you had. As you journal, I hope that you will be reminded of the beauty that may be found among the ashes.

This isn't going to be an easy book to read. It takes courage to begin the difficult process of releasing your story, but I pray that as we begin journaling together, we'll find comfort and encouragement from the women and families who have walked this rugged road before us. Ultimately, I pray that this sorrow will pull us closer to the God whose nail-marked hands hold tight to our stories, the One who has given us the gift of grief and who invites us to lift our tear-stained faces back towards Him.

Julie is a beautiful example of this. Over a one-and-a-half-year span, Julie and her husband experienced four unexplained, first-trimester losses. Picking up her pen and beginning to journal her way through a specific question, Julie felt frustrated. Looking back over the past year, she felt that God had not taken care of her. She began writing out the one and only situation in which she remembered seeing God's hand at work through the loss. Suddenly, she remembered another one and another one. Soon she had filled an entire page with the countless ways she had seen God take care of her. Julie says, "It was beautiful to realize that even though I had felt like God had left me alone, in reality, He had been very close and showed me His love through the most difficult times. Until I started writing them down, I had simply forgotten how many times these God-moments happened."

Throughout this book, we'll continue to look at many of the different aspects surrounding life after loss. We'll also hear loss stories from fellow grieving mothers. While I understand that some of these stories may feel difficult to carry, please know that I have placed them in here as a way to help release the stigma surrounding pregnancy loss and to glorify God together in the midst of our mutual loss. As we read these difficult stories, I pray that we would learn from one another's experiences and take comfort not only in our solidarity but, more importantly, in the God who is faithful throughout any and all circumstances. That being said, take this book at your own pace. Take time to reflect on these chapters and begin writing through the emotions and feelings that arise after reading them. At the end of each chapter, you'll find several journal prompts. The questions may not always be applicable, but like Julie, you may find yourself surprised by what feelings emerge. If something hits close to your heart, acknowledge it and begin working your way through it.

As we explore the depths of our grief and the challenges that coincide with life after loss, I hope that you will join a generation of women who are not afraid to talk about gritty, heartbreaking issues, women who share light and hope to the mourning and lost. Seeking God in the midst of our despair, I pray that we will learn to grieve authentically, with unclenched hands and hearts. There is hope here in this place of heaviness. Let's find it together.

Journaling Prompts
Telling Your Story

Take some time to begin writing out your story. If you're having trouble getting started, try to answer the following questions.

- What are some of your favourite memories from the pregnancy?

    (Depending on when you lost your little one, you may not feel that you even have "memories." That's okay. Instead, describe the desires that you dreamed of but never got to have, the pregnancy experiences that you feel robbed of, or the things you had imagined doing with this little one.)

- When did you know that you were losing your little one? How did you say good-bye? What did your grief feel like in that moment?

- What have you learned so far in this experience? How has it shaped (grown or broken) your faith? What encouragement do you need to hear to make it through this?

Chapter Two

Nobody Said So

A few years ago while scrolling through my Facebook newsfeed, I came across photos of a mother holding her newborn baby. Tears slid down her face as she gazed lovingly at the little one that had just been brought into the world. He was a bundle of cream-coloured blanket, all small and soft and beautiful. With his tiny lashes lying against rounded cheeks, he appeared to be asleep. But this wee one would never wake up. His name was Cornelius, and he was born still.

Cornelius is the son of Jennifer and her husband, Justin, a couple I met in college. They both have infectious laughter and a passion for sharing God's truth that permeates all areas of their lives. We didn't know each other very well, but even from afar it was clear to see their hunger for God's Word. Jennifer has graciously allowed me to share their story here in hopes that you too can see the echo of God's faithfulness throughout their loss.

Jennifer's Story

Jennifer was a week overdue with their first child. It had been an uncomplicated pregnancy, and at forty-one weeks along, the young couple were eager to find out when they would be induced. Arriving at their final prenatal appointment, everything felt routine: check the cervix, check for dilation, measure belly size … but when it came to the comforting whoosh of a heartbeat, there was only silence. Truthfully, Jennifer and her husband weren't worried. Throughout the pregnancy, the doctor had repeatedly experienced difficulty finding the heartbeat (particularly whenever Jennifer's husband was in the room). The couple chalked it up to the baby's usual stubbornness and thought nothing of the fact that they were being sent to the hospital for an additional check.

Jennifer says, "When we got into the van, we prayed and felt a great sense of peace flood over us. We were excited to go to the hospital and elated by the fact that the baby would finally arrive today."

But at the hospital, the silence lay thick and heavy. The fetal heart rate monitors were still, the ultrasound quiet. There was no movement, no heart fluttering or limbs bouncing. From her position on the narrow bed, Jennifer couldn't see her baby's image on the screen. Instead, she watched the hushed and drawn faces of her husband and doctor. "Up until this point, I had still been full of peace," Jennifer shares. "And then I heard the words, 'I'm sorry, the baby is gone.' Shock washed over me like a tidal wave."

The doctors had no explanations as to how this could have happened. Tears streamed down Justin's face while Jennifer remained in shock. All she felt was numb, so very numb. The hospital staff somberly left the room to give the grieving parents time and space to mourn.

Despite the medical staffs' attempts to persuade her otherwise, Jennifer was firm in her decision to have a caesarean. That evening, after receiving a partial sedative, Jennifer was taken in for surgery. She slept through most of it, waking to the news that they had a little boy. Her heart immediately overflowed with love for this precious child she'd carried for over nine months. Lying in a bassinet beside her, his face turned towards his parents, Jennifer says, "He looked like he was sleeping. He was so beautiful. How could I love someone who was dead so very much?"

It was midnight when they brought Jennifer from the operating table to a new room, and she was exhausted from the long, emotional day. The nurses brought their son to them and carefully gave him a bath. They placed him in his "going home" sleeper, wrapped him in a blanket, and passed the babe to his father. Jennifer and her husband named their son Cornelius. Jennifer says, "He was so big, yet so tiny. I couldn't hold him for long, because I was sore and he was so heavy. What was supposed to be a joyous day turned into the saddest day we will ever remember. His scent, touch, hair colour, eyes, and fingers will never be forgotten, but you'll always keep wondering what would he look like now? What would his personality be like?"

After spending some time with him, the parents noticed that Cornelius was turning purple. They had some photos taken with him: their son swaddled in a knit-blanket, Jennifer in a hospital gown and bed, and her husband standing beside them proud but heartbroken. With tears, they said their good-byes and wished for a longer time together. "When we left the hospital," Jennifer says, "we got into the van and noticed the car seat—the empty car seat. Then we came home to an empty house. The crib was empty. The rocking chair was not in use. It was surreal."

At the time, Jennifer's husband was reading through the Old Testament book of Exodus. The very next passage he read was the plague of the death of the firstborn son[8]. Jennifer says, "Providentially, God had placed that passage there at that time so that we might honour and glorify Him, knowing that He allowed the outcome. Even though it hurts and we still grieve, all we can do is groan at sin and praise God for His salvation."

> *For we know that the whole creation has been groaning together in the pains of childbirth until now. And not only the creation, but we ourselves, who have the first fruits of the Spirit, groan inwardly as we wait eagerly for adoption as sons, the redemption of our bodies. For in this hope we were saved. Now hope that is seen is not hope. For who hopes for what he sees? But if we hope for what we do not see, we wait for it with patience.*
>
> —Romans 8:22–25

Before she lost Cornelius, Jennifer says that she never knew how much a loss like this could hurt. "When people had miscarriages, it seemed as if they just went on with their lives. I was so ignorant of the pain that came along with pregnancy loss. It wasn't until I lost my son at forty-one weeks that I began to gain a better understanding of unconditional love like this."

---

[8] Exodus 11.

Jennifer's story was my first *real* introduction to the world of pregnancy loss. Their loss lay in my core like a rock, squeezing my heart at the sight of their grief. It hurts to see people you care about hurting. Beyond the very real images of pain and death sitting in my Facebook feed, this loss was also a bit of an awakening for me. It was the first time I realized that miscarriage and stillbirth aren't just topics found laced through history books and century-old family trees. They continue to occur in the here and now.

Growing up, miscarriages weren't talked about very frequently. In fact, I can only remember one conversation where it was purposefully brought up rather than hidden behind hushed whispers and church gossip. As a teen, I spent a majority of my summers floating in the milfoil-filled lake behind my grandparents' summer cabin. My grandad and I would paddle around on little Styrofoam buoys, our arms and legs skimming along the top of the water to avoid the sharp rocks beneath our feet. It was on one of these occasions that I learned about the uncle I never knew—a baby boy miscarried back in the sixties. With my grandmother napping on the porch and out of earshot, my grandad whispered of how he'd carefully spooned the perfectly formed baby out of the toilet into a glass jar and then drove it to the doctor's office. It seemed a relief for him to finally talk about the son he'd never known.

I was fourteen and, quite frankly, amazed by this long-secreted piece of family history. I felt as if I'd been let in on a secret club, as if someone had let me read fragmented stories from an old journal. But what my teenage-self failed to see was that this was more than just a piece of forty-year-old history. It's only now, looking back, that I can see the scars that lay beneath the surface. I hear my grandfather's hushed voice and know the wounds that lay tangled within his words.

It wasn't until I saw that precious, stillborn baby lying in a Facebook photo that I realized what this type of loss truly meant. The raw grief inscribed across the picture left me feeling shocked and uncomfortable. I was an outsider looking in on a crumbling world. The grief I felt for Jennifer and her husband was almost tangible, a scant taste of the sorrow that was to become so familiar in later years. But stronger still was the feeling of confusion. How could they so confidently post such an intimate photo of their deceased infant? The mother's arms were tightly wrapped around her son, but just thinking about holding my child's dead body left me feeling squeamish. With very few people normalizing the reality of infant loss, I couldn't wrap my head around the truths of that moment.

Would I hold my stillborn baby? I didn't have an answer, and I didn't think I'd ever need one. The picture disappeared into my ever-updating newsfeed and took my hypothetical ponderings with it. Even years later, during my own pregnancy, the word "stillbirth" never crossed my mind. After all, these are not the questions we like to think about.

Michelle, who lost her precious babe at nineteen weeks, agrees. She says that she was surprised by pregnancy loss. "When you find out you're pregnant, you begin to think about baby showers, labour, and delivery. You don't think about the possibility of not being able to live in those moments."

Most women have clear expectations for their pregnancy. Like Michelle, we expect to spend three full trimesters buying pregnancy books and setting up a nursery. We know that women in the mall will eye our ballooning bellies and stop to tell us about engorged breasts, colicky babies, and a never-ending parade of horrific labour stories. We're prepared to spend weeks busily researching and weighing possible options regarding genetic testing, home births, circumcision, and vaccinations. We download growth apps on our iPhones and eagerly wait to see what size of fruit the baby is this week. We mentally prepare ourselves for birth: for the forewarned pain and discomfort, third-degree tears, husbands who need laughing gas, and epidurals that don't work. We push aside our doubts and fears, focusing our attention elsewhere. We know the statistics but never imagine that they'll touch our lives.

But when you lose your child, you suddenly realize that you don't have answers to the questions being asked. From seemingly nowhere you're faced with an entirely different sort of pain. It's not childbirth—it's child loss. Your pregnancy has tumbled to an abrupt and resounding end, and you're walking blindly. A swarm of questions and details, mixed with agonizing pain and resounding fear, hover over you. Everyone told you how difficult breastfeeding was going to be, but no one ever warned you about *this*.

There are so many different aspects to baby loss that nobody talks about. We don't like uncomfortable topics. We inwardly cringe at the sound of the words "blood" or "cramps" in the same sentence as "woman." But by failing to normalize the stigmas surrounding miscarriage and stillbirth, we leave whole generations of women unprepared, alone, and unsure of whether or not it's okay to grieve. More so, as a church and as believers, we leave women unequipped and floundering without a strong theology of suffering. Is Christ still good in the midst of pain? Did God take away our child? Is it okay to question Him? To wrestle with doubts in the face of such tremendous pain?

As followers of Christ, we try to encourage others by rightly focusing on the hope we have for a heavenly tomorrow. But at the same time, we need to remember not to gloss over the everyday intricacies of living out that faith *now*. We need to teach newly bereaved families how to live in that tender place between the *now* and the *not yet*—the hope we have in Christ for tomorrow and the simultaneous hope and grace we have for right now in the midst of our earthly suffering. We can't overlook the fact that the practical aspects to our grief are often strong influencers of our spiritual walks—it is from here that our faith questions and challenges often arise.

The Physical Aspect of Loss

When Lexi experienced a miscarriage at five weeks, she was surprised. Living in a remote area of Africa with no access to powerful pain medication, she was caught off guard by the amount of physical pain she endured. No one had told her it would feel like that. Lexi says, "I have never hated the sensation of pain so much in my life. My pain was a constant reminder of the life lost."

Lexi isn't alone in this. Many women are surprised by the amount of physical pain a first-trimester miscarriage can produce. So why aren't we talking about miscarriage? Why aren't we sharing the messy, gritty stories of motherhood instead of just the Instagram perfect ones? No one ever talks about the fact that their first night of motherhood was spent lying on an uncomfortable hospital bed, their body silently screaming out for a lost baby. We're warned about the recovery times following a C-section, but no one tells us that the pain of pregnancy loss cuts a thousand times deeper than any incision on our abdomen. No one talks about autopsies and funeral homes, cremation, burials, or memorials. We may save money for extra baby onesies and diapers, but we don't talk about how it was spent on a small plot of earth and a bronze grave marker instead.

No one warns you that your miscarriage will be low-priority, or that you'll sit in the emergency room for hours, desperately trying to hold on to your baby. No one warns you that your miscarriage will be called a "spontaneous abortion" and that these clinical terms may cut deep. No one mentions the doctor who sits you down and tells you that "You can start trying again in a few months," all the while your wounded heart cries out for the baby that should have still been growing inside of you. We don't hear about the mother who had to watch the swirling remnants of her pregnancy pass away, her hopes and dreams sliding down the toilet in a clump of bloody water. Everyone prepares you for the post-pregnancy weight loss struggle, but no one tells you what to do when you're so numb you forget to eat. Or when your milk comes in and there's no baby to drink it. There are no baby manuals for what to do when you're forced to return a double stroller and matching car seats, the shop assistant's tears flowing freely alongside yours as you clutch the cashier's desk and sob. Everyone tells you to be prepared for the baby, but no one thinks about finding storage space for the crib that your husband so faithfully set up just a week prior.

No one ever talks about how they left the hospital empty handed, and because of that, we tend to think that the statistics surrounding pregnancy loss are wrong. The pregnancy pamphlets tell us that 15–25 per cent of pregnancies end in miscarriage, but we can only name one or two women who have ever talked about having one. It's not until you experience a loss yourself that you realize that these grieving mamas are all around you. Conscious of causing stress, society tiptoes down the fine line between awareness and fear but rarely lands on either side. We fail to offer support to mothers currently losing their little ones and instead put all our attention towards politely sidestepping the issue. The people who were so eager to give you parenting advice are now some of the first to shy away from discussion about your loss, and it can be a struggle to find people who acknowledge and talk openly about their own grief.

Many of us live as if loss is contagious. We walk through life with a "knock-on-wood" type of attitude: if we don't talk about it, then it won't happen to me! And yet by not talking about it, many of us who experience loss end up feeling isolated and alone. As fellow believers and brothers and sisters in Christ, we are not called to live this life of fear: "*The Spirit you received does not make you slaves, so that you live in fear again; rather, the Spirit you received brought about your adoption to sonship. And by him we cry, 'Abba, Father.'*" (Romans 8:15, NIV).

When loss touches upon our lives, we begin to see the world differently. We may find that our grief reflects the fragility of life and emphasizes our prior naivety. We don't emerge from this journey unchanged, but our identity in Christ is stronger than that of our former fearful selves. Still, this isn't an easy subject to talk about. Many women are unable to find the words to adequately portray the depth of their pain—this loss is personal, a love knit tightly to the heart. As grieving mothers, it's important for us to decide when and where we want to share this intimate pain. Not everyone needs to know our story. Not everyone is able to respect or protect it. However, we need to be sure that our fear is not the determining factor in whether or not we speak up about our loss.

For too many years, women have been asked to mute their grief. For generations, this subject has been quietly set aside, as mothers were taught to bottle up their grief and bury their wounds. There were no support networks—these things simply happened. Pregnancy loss was something to be hidden … a blighted mark to be repressed as quickly as possible. But this attitude is so, so wrong! Pregnancy and infant loss should not be taboo subjects. There is no shame to be held in infant loss, because *you did nothing wrong*.

This is one of the very real lies whispered to us after a loss: that *we* are at fault for this pain. That *our* body failed us and, because of that, we should be ashamed. That our scars somehow make us *less* than the other women who can carry babes to full-term. But none of these things are true. These lies have been whispered to women right from those early biblical moments in the garden, lies that say, "You have lost your value. You are worthless." And when it comes to pregnancy loss, these lies serve a larger purpose. By tricking and deceiving women into staying silent, the enemy has managed to convince entire generations of people that life still within the womb is essentially worthless too.

In Christ, there is freedom from these lies. His light punctures even the darkest of nights, breaking even the tightest bindings of guilt and shame. Following Christ doesn't mean that we won't encounter heartbreak—you and I are all too familiar with that fact by now—but it does mean that we can do *more* with our grief. We've come to Christ not because we "have it all together," but because we know that we're broken and that we need Him. In the age of social media, it's easy to want to try and portray life without blemish, but we are called to a life lived authentically. A life that embraces the story He's written and declares His glory in the midst of it. By opening up about our stories and our experiences, we declare Christ's pre-eminence over even the most difficult of situations. Only *His* truth is strong enough to break the walls of shame and deception that have been built around this topic.

Practically, by sharing our stories we also help to prepare those who come after us. At first glance, this may not seem like much. How can we ever prepare a mother for such a debilitating loss? Would we have listened, even if someone had told us what to expect? We all know that there will never be adequate warning for a moment like this. You will never be able to fully understand the pain until you walk through it. And yet by taking away the stigma and by creating a culture of awareness and common grief, we begin building supportive communities that allow women to grieve in a healthier manner. By talking about suffering, we give families the tools necessary to grieve differently than the rest of the world—to grieve with *hope*.

Although it's been several years, I often find myself reflecting back on that Facebook picture of Jennifer and Cornelius. A similar photo adorns my living room bookshelf, and I am now that woman. I too have had to answer the questions that no one wants to think about. Lying in a hospital bed, I was desperate to see my baby. There was no hesitation when the nurse asked if I wanted to hold my stillborn son. I wanted nothing more than to hold him, wrap my arms around the little boy I'd carried for seven months, and never let go. At that moment, I discovered the truth that had eluded me all those years ago: my love for him surpassed my fears.

There are a lot of things that no one tells us, but perhaps tragically, no one has ever told you how beautiful your baby would be. Even in death, despite his stillness and the trauma he's been through, he will be beyond precious. Whether you choose to see him or not, whether you hold a silent baby in your arms or an unrecognizable clump of tissue in your hands, your love will seep through. Her body is a shell, but you will hold her hand and whisper a lullaby in her ear. Your arms may be empty, but your heart will forever carry the weight of that beloved little child.

Journaling Prompts

What No One Ever Told You

These journaling prompts are questions that can be used to help you start journaling. Some days you may not need them, while other days you may rely on them completely. Let your grief guide your journaling. Answer as many or as few questions as you need to.

- List some of the experiences that you've had with grief thus far. Is there anything you wish you had known before this loss? Could anything have prepared you for this?

- Looking back at your experiences, write a letter to yourself on the day of your loss. Be open with yourself about the pain. Write about the things that no one warned you about. What words of encouragement do you have for yourself on that day? What do you know now that you didn't know then?

- What has this loss taught you about the fragility of life? In what areas of your life do you experience fear? How has this loss forced you to face your fears?

Chapter Three
The Right to Grieve

Springy earth clung to my sneakers as I watched an ant meander its way across my son's gravestone. A pile of cherry blossom petals covered the graves nearby, gently sweeping across half-melted candles and tinkling wind chimes. The world was new and shiny and shimmering with the promise of blue skies and brighter days. But the weather stood in sharp contrast to the wilting flowers and soggy teddy bears that usually marked this part of the cemetery. With a face contoured by black mascara streaks, I crouched beside the damp plot of dirt and wondered if perhaps it was time to stop grieving. Eight months had passed since the death of my son, and I worried that my grief was starting to draw out too long. Was it okay that I still missed him? That I still wanted to talk about him all the time? Was my grief starting to annoy those around me? Spring was here and, like the fresh breeze, maybe now it was finally time to move on.

In a world lacking positive grief role models, it was difficult to know what a "normal" grief time frame looked like. Perhaps as you read this, weeks or months or years into your loss journey, you too have found yourself worrying that this intense pain will never go away. Maybe you're questioning what "acceptable" grief looks like, or wondering how long you're "allowed" to grieve. You may struggle with feelings of guilt, worrying that you haven't grieved as hard as you should have, or perhaps you're feeling overwhelmed by the sheer volume of emotions that you've experienced. Maybe you too have found yourself kneeling beside a tiny baby's grave, wondering if perhaps it's just easier to stop thinking about the pain. If you've felt any of these things, know that you're not alone in these thoughts.

Grief is challenging to talk about because it's so intricate and unique to each of us. Our perceptions of loss are often strongly influenced by

Hollywood (which usually tells us that grief is here for one episode and gone another) and generational mores (which say that baby loss is not something to be publicly discussed). Due to the lack of honest and open conversation, grieving families and their relatives often hold unrealistic expectations as to what life after loss actually looks like. We may experience pressure from family members or co-workers to "move on" faster than we're ready, or we may feel that we don't have the right to mourn a baby lost before birth.

But let me tell you something, grieving mama: your pain will not fit into anyone else's timeline. This sweet child's life made a lasting impact on yours, and it's okay to recognize and acknowledge that. Whether you lost this precious babe in the first trimester or the third, you have the right to mourn for as loud and as long as *you* need to.

Tara-Lynn's Story

Tara-Lynn is one mother who has at times wondered whether or not her grief was valid. "Because I lost my baby at six weeks," she says, "I sometimes wondered whether or not I should feel sad about it. I've realized now that it doesn't matter how long you were pregnant—a loss is still a loss. No matter when your baby went home to be with the Lord, it's heartbreaking."

Tara-Lynn and her husband had been married for seven years and actively trying to conceive for three when they finally got pregnant. But just three days after that positive pregnancy test, Tara-Lynn started to spot. "I went to the doctor at the walk-in clinic and he said frankly to me, 'Well, if you're going to miscarry, then you're going to miscarry. There's nothing we can do about it.'" Upset by the doctor's brusque manner but optimistic that things could still turn out okay, Tara-Lynn headed home to rest. Feeling that this baby was a girl, Tara-Lynn and her husband named her Elliot and began calling her by name.

When she was still bleeding on Monday morning, Tara-Lynn went to emergency. After seven hours in the ER, and one failed vaginal ultrasound, she was sent home with a referral to an OB/GYN. Three days later, at exactly five weeks pregnant, another vaginal ultrasound confirmed that the egg sac was present and that it looked good. To celebrate this news, Tara-Lynn and her husband prepared to go away for a romantic couple's weekend. But by the time they arrived at the hotel on Friday evening, Tara-Lynn had started bleeding heavily. "I remember thinking that this was the end, but I still held on to faith. I couldn't understand why God would make us wait so long to get pregnant if He was only going to take her away."

The events that followed are vivid in Tara-Lynn's mind. The next day, heading to the bathroom at work, she found a devastating amount of blood. Cleaning it up, she kept working and faking a smile. "In hindsight," Tara-Lynn says, "I should have left work that minute, but I worked until later in the afternoon and then I went to the doctors' for another very painful ultrasound. There was too much blood, though, and they couldn't see what was going on."

Knowing it was over but not quite ready to accept it, Tara-Lynn went to bed that night hoping to wake up to a different scenario. Instead, she awoke in the early morning hours to intense cramping. Not wanting to wake her husband, she endured the pain alone on the couch for three hours, passing clot after clot. "By 4:00 a.m. the cramps and clots were gone, and I knew it was over."

Only it wasn't. Tara-Lynn went in for multiple blood tests to confirm that her HCG levels (a pregnancy hormone) were dropping, but they weren't. Tara-Lynn hadn't passed all of the pregnancy tissue, so a D&C[9] was scheduled for a couple of weeks later. Due to some unique complications with her uterus, the doctors were unable to collect any tissue during the D&C. Finally, at the end of March, Tara-Lynn was given a dose of methotrexate so that her body would rid itself of any tissue. Her period returned three months later and she remained hopeful that she'd get pregnant quickly, but month after month slowly slipped by without another positive test.

During the initial weeks and months following the loss, Tara-Lynn struggled to give herself permission to mourn. "I had no instruction manual or friends to tell me how to grieve, and I didn't feel understood enough to be very open about it at that time. I was the first in my friend group to experience a pregnancy loss, and I knew nothing about it; no one ever spoke to me about it. Since I'd never seen grief modelled in a healthy manner, I

---

9   Dilation and curettage (or a D&C) is a procedure that may be used to scrape and clear the uterus after a miscarriage.

stumbled my way through it." Tara-Lynn also says that she was surprised by how quickly she had bonded with the baby. "From the moment I found out about Elliot, I began talking to her and dreaming of a life with her. I thought that losing her so early on wouldn't be, or shouldn't be, so hard—but it was! While I still think about her often, I rejoice, as I choose to believe that God's plan is sovereign."

A year after the loss of Elliot, the doctors discovered that Tara-Lynn had a unicornuate (half) uterus with only one tube and one ovary. Paired with a very low egg count, this meant that Tara-Lynn could go into menopause before she turned thirty-five. Tara-Lynn says that she continued to feel out of place and pressured to have a baby. It seemed as if everyone was pregnant except for her. Due to their ongoing struggle with infertility, Tara-Lynn feared that this miscarried pregnancy had been her only chance, and she worried that another opportunity may never come again. "After miscarrying and struggling with infertility, I felt robbed of everything. I felt like I would never have a child, but after a couple of years of grieving, I eventually came to a place where I was able to accept God's plan. I felt that my husband and I could still have a great life, even without kids."

Almost a year and a half after the loss of her little girl, Tara-Lynn saw another positive pregnancy test. This time, they got to bring the baby home. In 2016, Tara-Lynn and her husband gave birth to a beautiful son, born early but healthy at thirty-four weeks.

Three years after her miscarriage, Tara-Lynn still remembers the loss vividly but feels as though her heart has healed. "I'll never forget Elliot, and she will always have a place in my heart. Because of that, I acknowledge special dates and feel sad meeting babies with her name, but ultimately I know that the Lord is in control. As painful as this experience was, I'm not the only one who has gone through it. I didn't know that then, but now that I do, I'm glad I can use our story to help support others going through this heartbreaking experience."

When it comes to grief, we all find ourselves facing different pressures or influences. Like Tara-Lynn, you may have struggled to give yourself permission to fully grieve. Or perhaps like fellow mom Lexi, you've found yourself undergoing a tug-of-war of mixed pressures. Lexi says that after experiencing a miscarriage, she felt pressure from the infant and pregnancy loss community to grieve longer and more deeply. Conversely, she has also felt pressure from the culture at large to not grieve at all.

At some point throughout your grief journey, you too may have felt the weight of any one of these pressures. Grief is a confusing and challenging road to walk, and these additional stressors and misunderstandings can be exhausting. But when it comes to knowing "how" to grieve, there are two important things to keep in mind.

1. Your Grief Timeline Belongs to YOU and You Alone

I've always found water to be a comforting metaphor for my grief. Like the ocean, this pain ebbs and flows with the tide—there's no set timeline or order. Recently while walking along the beach out front of my summer cabin, I picked out bits of a broken beer bottle lying amongst the rocks. On its own, this fractured bottle tossed overboard by a careless boater has the potential to cause great pain. Yet by the time it's washed up on my beach, its sharp edges have been smoothed and buffeted by the water to create something pleasant and smooth. These bits of sea glass are treasured and beheld by beachcombers across the world—not because they're whole, but because there's something special about how they've been transformed. Like this shattered bottle, we do not emerge from our grief the same way we went in, yet there's beauty in this brokenness.

Your grief experience will never align exactly with anyone else's. Sometimes this grief is gentle and calming, reassuring in its steady waves. Other times it has all the force of a category-one hurricane, battering and overpowering everything in its path. The emotions you feel belong to you alone. There's no correct way to grieve. There's no set timeline to follow. But while we know this in theory, it can be difficult to let ourselves truly soak in our grief and take the time we need to work through it. Not knowing the intensity of grief that awaits us, it can be challenging to let go and simply embrace.

One fellow grieving mama, Joy, has experienced seven different losses at varying stages throughout her pregnancies. Like many other women,

Joy's biggest struggle with the grieving process has been knowing when and if she has grieved for long enough. She says, "I feel pressured by people to 'snap out of it' and 'move on.' I've struggled to allow myself to grieve when and where I want."

Recently, social media has been an excellent platform for women to share and express the intensiveness of their grief, but this hasn't always been the case historically. Those outside of the baby loss community may not understand why you're still grieving. Due to generational or cultural differences, or a simple lack of grief understanding, your friends and family may not be as supportive or compassionate as you'd hoped they would be. The countdown timer they have allotted for your grief has now hit zero. Most often, these friends or co-workers genuinely believe that they have your best interests at heart. By telling you to "be strong" or "move on," they're hoping to help you move past the pain and heartache. Loss mom Dulci has experienced this first hand. She says, "I have at times felt pressure to grieve faster and get 'better,' but I know that it's just coming from my loved ones' desire to protect me from pain and to see me happy."

This pressure to move on doesn't always come from those around us: sometimes it comes from within. Perhaps like me, you've found yourself kneeling at a damp grave, wondering when on earth these tears are going to stop. Maybe you just want the pain to go away, or you feel frustrated for not grieving as quickly as other mothers. If you lost a child early in the pregnancy, you may feel as if you don't have a right to mourn this baby as long as a mother who lost her child at full-term. This self-applied pressure can be just as damaging as outside pressures.

But no matter what kind of stressors you may find yourself facing, it's important not to rush through your grief because you feel it's what you're "supposed" to do. You should never be made to feel guilty for mourning a longer or shorter period of time than those around you. Hurrying or bottling up your grief only hinders you overall.

While the motto "be strong and move on" may look nice on paper, it often cripples and deters one's grief instead of bracing and supporting it. Instead of sharing or acknowledging our pain, this motto tells us to hide it. When we're told to "buck up," we're being denied the right to grieve. We live in an orderly world of schedules and day-timers, meetings and agendas, but our emotions are not so easily filed away. We may try to avoid dealing with our grief, but we cannot hide from this pain forever; eventually, it will begin to bubble up and overflow.

Yes, it hurts to be vulnerable and it hurts to feel weak, but the battle wounds that have burned themselves upon our hearts aren't something to be ashamed of. Strength doesn't mean that we have conquered and vanquished our grief. Strength is found in the messy, everyday struggle to face our fears and wade through the sorrow. This strength to face our grief cannot come from within. It comes when we lay our battered bodies at the feet of the cross and, in our weakness, cry out to the heavenly Father. This is what it means to truly embrace our grief. These are the days when the weight of the world bruises your shoulders and tests your endurance, but there is hope for a brighter tomorrow. Because of Christ and the redeeming work He accomplished on the cross, we can hold tight to the promise of a tomorrow without death or tears: *"He will wipe away every tear from their eyes, and death shall be no more, neither shall there be mourning, nor crying, nor pain anymore, for the former things have passed away"* (Revelation 21:4).

Until that joyous day, we will cry and we will ache over this seemingly impossible separation from our little ones. Grief takes time and patience to work through (something we all are admittedly not very good at). This doesn't mean that we allow our grief to conquer or defeat us, but simply that we're not confined by impractical expectations or time limitations. As the waves of grief flow, acknowledge what you're feeling and trust in the God who created us to love passionately and to bond deeply—the same God who does not diminish our right to grieve and mourn but allows us to find hope amidst the sorrow.

2. Not All Loss Is Equal, but All Loss Is Still Loss

Katie's Story: When Katie found out at her twelve-week scan that she was expecting identical twins, she felt as if she could burst with happiness. She and her fiancé hadn't been trying to conceive, but Katie was so excited to be a mother. Buying clothes and cribs, the couple eagerly planned a nursery and talked about matching names. The doctors monitored the pregnancy closely, and at her eighteen-week scan, Katie experienced her first taste of the incredible ups and downs that were to come. The doctors announced that Katie was carrying two precious little girls, and simultaneously told Katie that the twins were in need of emergency surgery. Scared and anxious, the young couple immediately piled into their car and drove seven hours to a hospital that could complete the surgery. Katie says, "It was the scariest moment of my life, knowing how vulnerable my baby girls were and how the next few days could change our lives forever." The morning after the ultrasound, Katie underwent laser ablation surgery. The procedure was a success, and Katie was overjoyed by the instant improvement of both twin's health. But this good news didn't last long.

A few days following the surgery, Katie became very ill and was admitted back into her local hospital with a serious infection. When the infection triggered pre-term labour, Darcy-Mae and Penelope Rose Nicol were born still at just twenty-one weeks. Katie says, "They were so small and perfect. I didn't know that I could feel such conflicting pride and heartbreak in one day. I miss my little girls with every fibre of my being, but I'm so glad that I was blessed enough to carry them."

After the loss of her girls, Katie says that she felt a lot of pressure to grieve quickly but that the extent of grief didn't truly hit her until five months in. When Katie's close friend had two first-trimester miscarriages, Katie was also quick to realize a common misconception that often accompanies pregnancy loss. After her friend's six-week and eleven-week miscarriages, Katie had a difficult time understanding the depths of the other mama's sorrow. "I felt as though she hadn't lost half as much as me. She never bought them clothes, planned their names, or even gave birth to them. I didn't understand why she was so sad. I now realize that whether you've just found out about your baby or you lose them at full term, your grief is always valid. It's not a competition as to who has lost more."

These types of stories are difficult to share. They're messy and vulnerable but so important to hear. If we don't begin normalizing conversations about pregnancy loss, we miss out on vitally important keys to understanding grief. Katie's story touches upon a beautiful and important aspect to pregnancy loss: not all loss is equal, but all loss is valid. It's easy for us to begin comparing our grief to those around us. We may begin downplaying and devaluing our own experience, or we may feel that someone else's loss should be less painful or drawn out than ours. Another loss mother, Meg, says, "I feel that when I tell people that my loss happened at twenty weeks, and their loss happened earlier, they say things like, 'I know I didn't have something *so serious* happen to me, but …' Similarly, I find myself saying this type of statement to someone who lost their baby closer to full term." This pattern of thinking is easy to fall into. In a world that judges the validity of human life based on a baby's ability to survive outside of the womb, we may struggle to understand why we (or those around us) grieve so deeply for early losses. We may find ourselves unintentionally basing the legitimacy and intensiveness of our grief on the number of weeks we were given with our child.

After my first miscarriage, I too found myself facing this dilemma. I began comparing the intensity of my pain and the length of my grief to that of my stillbirth. I ached and agonized over the fact that I wasn't grieving this eight-week miscarriage to the same extent that I'd grieved my thirty-one-week stillbirth. I wanted to feel this pain as deeply as I'd felt my first loss, but the truth was that I just wasn't. My head told me that the losses should be equal, no matter the length of time that I'd spend with my babies. I believed that they each deserved to be mourned with the same depth of intensity and purpose, and I was angry at myself for what I perceived to be a lack of emotion. This miscarried babe was just as much my child as my stillborn son! So why did the loss of her brother scorch and shred my heart, while her loss just left me feeling frozen and out of sorts? But in my desire to prove my love for this baby, I'd missed out on a crucial piece of understanding: not all losses *are* the same.

Miscarrying at eight weeks, I never got to feel the budding flutters of new life, or the full term, rib-cracking kicks and turns. We were still playing "guess-the-gender" games, and there were no ultrasound photos or lists of names sticky-tacked to the fridge. No one except my husband knew that I was expecting. I had no nausea, no pregnancy symptoms, and my belly bump was solely comprised of too many chocolate chip cookies for breakfast. To top it all off, I was so busy chasing a toddler around the house, I barely had time to "feel" pregnant. There's no doubt that, for me, losing Landon at thirty-one weeks was a much heavier blow than my first trimester losses. The grieving process following the stillbirth was much longer and more challenging for me to work through.

BUT (and this is a *big* but!) just because I didn't feel the same intensity of grief after my first miscarriage doesn't mean that I loved this baby any less or wanted it any less. It doesn't mean that I don't have the right to grieve her too. I didn't know this little one as well as I knew my son. I didn't feel her move or watch her dance on an ultrasound machine, but I still lost someone very, very special to me. No matter how far along you are, the loss of a child is still *the loss of a child*.

For those who identify as followers of Christ, we understand the sanctity of life. We believe that all life is created *by* God *for the glory of* God. In this, we find the beautiful freedom to mourn even the earliest of miscarriages—to acknowledge that life existed at conception and to know that it is okay (good even!) to mourn and weep over the loss of this precious child. In the act of mourning those that the world fails to recognize, we place ourselves under the sovereignty of Christ, acknowledging the creator who is at work in *all* things from the very start. This very same understanding that gives us the freedom to grieve also gives us the freedom to rejoice.

Rejoice seems a strange word to see in a book about pregnancy loss, I know. James 1:2 tells us to *"Count it all joy, my brothers, when you meet trials of various kinds."* But joy? Rejoicing? How do we get to that place amidst the searing pain of a miscarriage? How do we rejoice in this suffering and agony when our very hearts hurt to beat? When our lungs cry out for breath, and our wombs ache with the futility of it all?

If this is where you're at, let me first and foremost encourage you to cast your eyes upon Jesus. When we seek His will and glory above all else, we can find joy in even the direst of circumstances. We stand before Him with the freedom to fully grieve but also with the freedom that comes with knowing that there is more to this story than what we see. The God who has stood so faithfully throughout time will not and *cannot* abandon His children in times of darkness and shadow. Although we don't now understand, we know that there will come a day when we see clearly—that while God never delights or revels in death, His hand is still at work, even here.

This is why, as Christians, we do not grieve as the world does. We do not grieve with *hopeless* abandon, nor do we brush off a miscarriage as a piece of insignificant tissue. We grieve with the assurance of a God who is in control, who is ever faithful, and who is actively present in this situation.

Because of this, we don't have to trouble ourselves with the *way* we grieve a pregnancy loss, with the way it *looks* or *feels*. I have now had four miscarriages, and I've responded differently to each and every one of them. The length of gestation is not the sole factor in determining the magnitude of grief. Grief looks different from mother to mother and pregnancy to pregnancy, but reacting differently to each loss does not make one of "greater importance" than the other. I love my babies deeply, miss them all profoundly, and would have given anything to have gotten to keep them. Mourning them differently did not change their value. Loss is loss, whether you lose a child in your first trimester or your third.

Amy experienced a chemical pregnancy at five weeks, but when her friend also went through a miscarriage, she too found herself comparing their grief. Amy shares, "My friend also lost her baby, and her miscarriage was a lot more traumatic. She worked through her grief in a very different way than I did. At the time, I sort of felt like it was a little over the top, but then I took a step back and realized that it's really not my place to judge, especially another grieving mother. I now see it as a way that she grieves, and it helped her process."

I think it's natural for us to want to compare loss. We wonder why one mama grieves harder than another, or why one type of loss hurts for longer. We question whether we should be grieving *more* or whether we're a horrible mother for not grieving as long as someone else. We try to comfort ourselves or others by thinking, *At least I lost this baby early on*, or *At least my experience wasn't as bad as another mama's*. But there is no "at least" in this situation. These little ones are more than just the number of weeks spent circling in our wombs; they are our children.

Mandy is another grieving mother who found herself comparing her grief to that of those around her: "I was part of a loss support group where a lot of women had an early loss and were completely devastated by it. I found it very difficult to relate to them in this way. I felt that they had no idea what loss really was compared to what I had gone through. I've since realized that everyone grieves differently, and it wasn't productive for me to compare myself to others."

Mandy is oh-so-right. Comparing our grief is *not* productive for us or for those around us. In a time when we need relationships most, we let our emotions isolate us from the very women who can speak into our lives in a meaningful way (and vice-versa). We devalue our own grief or the grief of those around us and perpetuate feelings of inadequacy or guilt. Worse yet, this comparison game deceives us into taking our eyes off Christ. Rather than embracing *our* grief as a means to draw nearer to God, we become distracted by a journey that doesn't belong to us. How can we fully live out Christ's love to those around us when we're stuck in a place of comparison?

This is something that takes time to wrestle with. The freedom from comparing whose loss is "bigger" can only come from settling our gaze firmly on Christ and allowing Him to redeem and restore our own feelings from those of inadequacy and guilt. I no longer carry guilt for mourning my stillborn son for longer than I did my miscarried babes. I had to intentionally choose to set that guilt aside and grieve each of my losses *as I needed to*. Each baby is a special God-given gift, and each of us needs to mourn our children as we feel best. Beyond the fact that there is no pain like the death of a child, one loss simply cannot compare to another. At four weeks or at forty, a loss is a loss.

Journaling Prompts
Your Right to Grieve

- Do you believe that you have the right to grieve for as long as you need to? Why or why not? What are some things that may prevent you from mourning for as long as you need to? Is there anything that you feel like you should be doing but aren't?

- What has been your biggest struggle with grief thus far? What frustrates you about the grieving process?

- How do you feel about the idea, "Not all loss is equal, but all loss is still loss?" How does that affect your thoughts on grief?

Chapter Four

Playing the Blame Game

A surge of heat lies deep within you, a fiery ache that simmers against the surface, ever present and ever growing stronger. Your heart beats heavy and loud in your ears as you fight the rising, unrelenting anger. The tension builds until something finally snaps and you find yourself releasing a flood of unintentional, emotional sludge onto some unsuspecting individual. The anger feels so real, so intense. Surely, something *must* be responsible for this pain. Someone must be held accountable for this loss!

After the death of a loved one, anger can be a startling but not uncommon response to grief. Many individuals are surprised by the intensity and passion that ripples threateningly under their weary exterior. Sometimes this frustration is clearly defined, while at other times you may be unsure as to what or whom you're truly angry at. As intense as these emotions are, they may not even feel logical.

Sarah, who we met in chapter one, touches upon some of the anger that can arise after a miscarriage or stillbirth when she says, "I was so angry after our second loss. It took a couple of months before I even tried to figure out why I was angry—or for that matter, *who* I was angry at. I was angry at the situation. I was angry because we wanted a child so badly. I was angry at God for allowing such a horrible thing to happen to me again. I was angry at myself for being so angry. It was a vicious cycle. I had to rely on my faith to let those angry feelings subside. Specifically, I focused on the promises of Revelations 21:4—that one day there will be no more sadness, pain, or sorrow."

If you've felt emotions similar to Sarah, you're definitely not alone. Maybe some of that anger has been directed inwards, generating feelings of self-blame and shame. In your search to find answers to the great question why, you may find yourself battling a constant stream of "what ifs" that can linger for months or years after the loss:

"What if I'd gone to the hospital earlier?"

"What if I hadn't lifted that heavy box the day before the miscarriage?"

"What if the doctor had noticed something on my earlier scan?"

"What if I hadn't had that cup of coffee?"

"If I had done something differently, would my baby still be with me?"

Besides harbouring guilt towards ourselves, these feelings of blame may begin falling onto those around us. Individuals such as our doctors, ultrasound technicians, or family or friends are all probable recipients of our frustrations and anger. It's also likely that some of your anger or frustration has been directed towards God. You may find yourself questioning, "How could a loving God allow my baby to die?" or "How could this possibly be a part of His *good* plan?"

When Rose lost her baby at just sixteen weeks, she says that she felt very angry. "Right after I lost my son, I began blaming myself. I felt like it was my fault, and I was very angry at God. How could a loving, wondrous God dangle something so precious in front of my face and then just rip it away? What made it worse is the fact that I still have no idea what caused the loss. Was it the medication that my psychiatrist told me was safe but absolutely wasn't? Was it the baby's father, who pushed me into sex constantly and didn't care how I felt about it? Was it my diet? I blamed my psychiatrist for lying to me, I blamed the baby's father for using me, and I blamed myself. All I felt was anger and hurt."

Reading Rose's words, it's easy to see the pain that has echoed across her story. Many of us hesitate to voice these feelings out loud for fear of how we may come across. But Rose's words touch upon four key areas in which many of us struggle with placing blame after loss: ourselves, medical professionals, those who are closely linked to us, or God. In this chapter, we're going to explore and unpack those a little bit in an attempt to seek restoration in those areas. As we look closely at the following four places of blame, open up a blank journal page and begin jotting down any emotions or experiences that come to mind. Prayerfully ask God to reveal any anger, bitterness, or guilt that you've been holding on to, and reflect on some ways in which you can begin to release and let go of those emotions.

1. We Blame Ourselves

After my son's stillbirth, I immediately began scolding myself: "Why did I wait to go to the hospital? If I knew something was wrong, why did I wait so long to get help?"

For weeks afterwards, I struggled and fought against feelings of guilt and responsibility for his death. I knew it was irrational. There was nothing else I could have done to save my son. The morning after his death, I lay in my hospital bed with glassy-eyes and a hollow heart and listened as the doctors reassured me that I had done everything right. I had been quick and determined in my decisions, giving everything in my power to ensure his safety. I had given my best, but my son still died.

The logical knowledge that I was not at fault didn't make it any easier to release my guilt. The feelings of self-accusation and remorse lay like hot coals in my gut, blistering against my conscience and burning their way through my self-reflection. In order to move forward, I needed to actively wrestle against the blame. I needed to figure out why I felt the way I did.

I began to ask myself whether or not I could have done anything differently. Realistically, could my actions have created a different outcome? I tormented myself with the idea that I could have saved Landon. If I'd gone to the hospital on Tuesday rather than waiting until Thursday, would I have come home with two babies in my arms instead of just one? While there are days I wish for a DeLorean time machine, there's only one reality that lies before me. I will never know for sure whether or not my actions could have changed my story, but I do know that *this* is what I've been given. I cannot change my past, but I can decide whether or not to release its hold over me.

Julie says, "Often I blame myself and my own body for my losses. I struggle with thinking that, somehow, I'm not good enough to be a mom, and that's why God has chosen for me to not be able to have kids. One of the best things to help me easily reject this lie occurred when my husband heard me say it and responded with, 'You know that *(insert celebrity name)* has kids, right?' With this offhand comment, he clearly rebutted the lie that

I'd been telling myself—that you had to be a perfect person with perfect motherly skills in order to be able to have a child. So now when I start to get sad about this lie, I think of that particular celebrity and pray for her and her kids."

Tara-Lynn has also felt those sinking feelings of guilt after loss, and says, "I remember thinking that the miscarriage was my fault because I had been drinking coffee prior to knowing I was pregnant. Though I'm only a casual coffee drinker, I was terrified to drink coffee for a long time, thinking that was the reason I had lost the baby. Time and accurate medical information have helped me to release these guilty feelings."

Maybe you're reading this today and feeling like I did, or like Julie or Tara-Lynn. You're worried that *you* are somehow responsible for your loss. You feel that *your* body failed you, or that *you* did something wrong. You feel that you're undeserving of motherhood or that it's some sort of "bad karma" for something you did in your past. You've heard lies whispered by the enemy and collected misinformation and old wives' tales from generations before. You know the truth, but the guilt still eats away at your insides, creating a whirling mess of anxiety and regret. So in case no one has ever told you this, let me say it now: You are not to blame for this. This is not your fault.

Pregnancy is one of the few areas in life where we're faced with the stark realization of helplessness. We are not in control of the way our child looks, the number of fingers on their hands, or the strands of DNA woven into their cells. When we blame ourselves, we fail to recognize that we are not the ones in control of life and death. We are not in control of their health, IQ level, or personalities—only God carries that level of authority. We may carry our babes in the womb, but we cannot make their hearts beat. Realizing that I wasn't in control was the first step in laying my guilt before God and letting Him lift that weight for me. I had to realize that it was not up to me to save my children. Just as we cannot fully protect our children outside of the womb, we cannot protect them inside either. As deep and as whole as my love for them was, I could not give them life. Thankfully, we serve the God who offers us more than just physical bones and breath—He offers us life eternal.

In Jeremiah 1:5, God tells the prophet, *"Before I formed you in the womb I knew you, before you were born I set you apart ..."* (NIV). God knows our children, just as He knows us. He sees them before they're formed and knows the length of their days from the start. While He could have left us to grieve without hope, He decided to do something much, much bigger. Two thousand years before this child was formed within you, God had already put into action the ultimate rescue plan: a plan that does not fade or wash away with time, a plan that is permanent rather than temporary. While death comes to us all, in Him is the promise of no life lived without purpose.

2. We Experience Anger Towards Those around Us

"Because you're too far dilated, I cannot proceed with the surgery. You can either stay here in the hospital and wait for labour to begin naturally, or we'll give you medication to induce labour and terminate the pregnancy." The doctor's words rang harshly against Meg's ears. At twenty weeks pregnant, she had been sent home from the hospital the night before and told to return in the morning. Now that she was here again, it seemed to be too late.

Meg and her husband were living in Northwestern China when she became pregnant for the second time. Their first pregnancy had been smooth and complication-free—their daughter born at thirty-nine weeks in a Chinese hospital in their town. Meg looked forward to a similar experience with their second pregnancy too, but at twenty weeks, Meg noticed that something was wrong. Heading into the ER, Meg was told that she'd need a cervical cerclage[10] but would have to wait until morning. She and her husband returned home for a restless night's sleep, only to discover the next morning that she was now too far dilated for the procedure.

Meg chose to stay in the hospital and wait until she went into labour naturally. The following day, Meg asked a friend to place her in contact with another doctor for a second opinion. The doctor lived in a town four hours away and agreed to transfer Meg by ambulance to another hospital. After a middle-of-the-night ambulance ride, Meg arrived at the hospital in the

---

10 Also known as a "cervical stitch." This procedure helps hold the cervix closed to prevent pre-term labour.

morning but had to wait until evening for an empty operating room. A cerclage was finally placed and Meg was put on bedrest for a week.

At the end of that week, Meg began to show signs of infection. Her water broke, and Meg went into labour. After delivering and losing a beautiful daughter, the nurses brought a black plastic bag to put their child into. Declining, Meg and her husband laid their daughter in a box that they had decorated with some friends who were caring for Meg's older daughter. When Meg was released from the hospital a week later, they buried their tiny baby girl and had a small funeral. Their family members still in North America were unable to be with them.

Meg says, "I had many months of grieving and really hating Chinese culture, as I blamed things in the culture for us losing our daughter. I specifically felt as if the Chinese medical professionals hadn't done enough to save my daughter. It was a fast way of learning how this culture treats early life. Because of China's one child policy, my Chinese friends didn't understand why I'd want to keep a pregnancy where something was 'wrong.' Oftentimes, mothers in China throw away their stillborn child and don't want to see them. It's part of their grieving process to keep those emotions far away: a mother would need strength to go back home without a baby and to get her body back to a healthy state. It took me months to forgive the medical professionals for wanting to throw away my baby and to forgive my Chinese friends for not wanting to grieve my daughter with me. They wanted me to forget her so that I could get healthy myself and would ask questions like, 'Why do you want to name your daughter?' or 'Why did you bury her?' 'Why are you so sad? You can have another.'"

Through this situation, Meg found beauty in the ability to be fully honest with God. "I had to tell Him how angry I was that my daughter was dead. I told Him how angry I was that the people around me didn't seem to respect her life. Later on, God brought about change and allowed me to understand the Chinese culture better. He helped me to understand God's heart for us mothers as we grieve the loss of a baby. Being honest with God about my grief turned into freedom: I felt free to be angry and make it known to Him instead of feeling like I had to deal with it in a 'good' manner."

Meg refused to shy away from her anger and sadness, and in doing so, was able to embrace her grief in a positive way. "Embracing grief means fully telling God what I felt instead of waiting for the 'good' emotions to come," she says. "If I didn't feel the fullness of the emotions, I would have been stuck and lost as to how to go on to the next step of grief."

Anger at those around us isn't something that we like to talk about very often. It isn't pretty, and when you begin to break it down, it often isn't rational. This is why I love Meg's story so much: her honesty and vulnerability reach deep into the hearts of so many grieving women, bringing words to the emotions we're sometimes too afraid to voice. Oftentimes, we're afraid to talk about "negative" emotions for fear of judgement or condemnation, but like Meg, we too can find freedom in honesty.

During the grieving process, it often feels easier to direct our anger at something or someone tangible rather than having to face the fact that there's just no satisfactory answer as to *why* this happened. With the weight of guilt pulling on our shoulders and gnawing at our stomach, we may try to subconsciously lighten the load by sliding these accusing emotions onto our friends and family. Like Meg, our anger may stem from cultural or generational differences, or perhaps just from a simple lack of understanding. We may feel frustrated with specific individuals or society as a whole.

This anger is a natural response to grief, and like all other emotions it has been created by God. While our anger can erupt from sinful roots and selfish desires, there's nothing wrong with anger in and of itself. The problem arrives, however, when our fury is misplaced and directed at the people around us. During a time when love and support are most important, we may accidentally hinder relationships by building up walls of guilt, anger, and bitterness.

Like most "good Christian girls" growing up within the church, I was taught the importance of swallowing tempers and masking irritations. But when it comes to grief, acknowledging these feelings of frustration and rage is an important first step in releasing it. Anger can be very helpful in exposing pent up emotions—don't bury the dirt, deal with it. Take the time you need to scream, cry, go for a long run, sit down and spend time in prayer, or head to the gym and sweat it out on a punching bag. It's difficult to be angry at death and sin. It's easier to be angry at *someone*.

Scriptures do not deny our feelings of anger and pain, but while the Bible recognizes our emotions, we need to be careful that in our hurt we do not cross into sin. Psalm 4:4 tells us to *"Be angry, and do not sin; ponder in your own hearts on your beds, and be silent."* Apart from damaging close relationships, anger towards others can be detrimental to our personal grieving process. In the white-hot moments of frustration and fury, our vision can be so focused on others that we become blind to our own grief. When we let our anger crash down upon those around us, we miss the chance to sit down, work *through* our frustrations, and release them. By holding onto our anger, we give up the opportunity for God to restore the agony and bring healing to the relationships with those around us.

3. We Blame Those Who "Should Have Known Better"

At thirty-one weeks pregnant with twin boys, I called my doctor's office and left a teary-sounding voicemail asking whether or not I should head to the hospital. I'd been feeling reduced movements for two days, but like most first-time moms, I'd spent that time googling and second-guessing myself. For the rest of the day my phone was glued to my palm as I sweated and prayed, waiting for a call back. Ten hours later, my phone finally buzzed its generic ringtone and I heaved a sigh of relief at the receptionist's voice— she apologized, she had *forgotten* to check her answering machine.

My son was born still less than two hours later. Had he been born earlier that day, he may have survived. In the days following my son's death, some of my anger fell upon (what I felt to be) this medical assistant's incompetency. I was angry at those ten hours I'd spent at home, each passing minute the difference between life and death. But as frustrating as the situation was, this receptionist was not the one to blame. She had not killed my son: twin-to-twin transfusion syndrome had. And while she may have played a very small part in a long list of things that hadn't gone ideally, it wasn't fair or healthy for me to continually blame her.

Another twin mama, Emily, says, "I did blame my doctors a little after the loss of our twins: I should have been more closely monitored than I was. Even so, nothing really could have been done. Once a little time had passed, I no longer blamed anyone, because it simply wasn't logical."

Some of you also experienced medical slips and incompetency within your pregnancies: there was the ultrasound that should have been read differently, a fatal misdiagnosis, or an incorrect call during birth. I know several families who feel that their little one would still be alive had it not been for a medical error—and that is just oh-so heartbreaking to hear.

The truth is that there are occasions where doctors miss things and end up making genuine and horrifying mistakes—faults that they have to live with too. In the occasions where someone may truly be "at fault" for the loss of our little one, we may feel that we need them to acknowledge their responsibility and/or to be held accountable for it in a court of law. If this is the case, proceed prayerfully and deliberately, continually seeking God for restoration and healing. Remember that restoration doesn't mean avoiding justice or encouraging negligence within the medical community—it simply means that you refuse to allow anger and bitterness to control your life. How this plays out will look different for all of us. We need to prayerfully decide what actions bring us closer to healing and what simply causes more hurt.

4. We Experience Anger Towards God

When Joy became pregnant with her rainbow baby[11] and then lost that little one too, she says, "I was so mad at God. I was finally at peace with not having any more kids, but when I got pregnant again, I thought that maybe this was my reward for being so faithful and positive after my previous losses. When God took that rainbow baby home too, I was ticked. Why would He do that to me? He knows how much I love kids and want more babies. Why would He snatch it away yet again?"

After the loss of a child, many Christians find themselves suddenly struggling with this fourth category: we grow angry and begin to blame God or question His goodness.

"If God is good, why did He let my baby die?"

"Wasn't He strong enough to save my child?"

---

[11] Rainbow Baby: A term common amongst loss parents, indicating the pregnancy that follows after a miscarriage, stillbirth, neonatal death, or infant loss. Just as a rainbow brings light and hope following a storm, so does a rainbow baby. (A rainbow baby does not replace a previous loss, nor does the term imply that the miscarried baby itself was a storm to be gotten over.)

"Everyone tells me that God has a plan for my life. But how can I trust that He has my best interests at heart when He took my infant away from me?"

Most of us would be lying to say that these sorts of thoughts hadn't crossed our mind at least once. And there's nothing wrong in wrestling with tough questions. It's okay to ask God why. "Why did I lose my baby but that woman in the NICU experiencing withdrawal got to keep hers?" or "So many women don't want to be pregnant, but I did. It's not fair that I didn't get to keep my baby! Why did this happen to me?" These questions are phrased in countless ways in almost every pregnancy loss group, but boil them all down to the essentials and you'll come away with the same question: "Why did *my* child have to die?"

For Joy, it took a lot of prayer and self-reflection to work through her anger. "I was just tired of being mad all the time. It was exhausting, and that wasn't the kind of person I wanted to be. I didn't want to be bitter. I've always prided myself on having a strong faith, but this definitely tested it. I was angry and didn't understand why. It took time—a lot of time—but I'm not angry anymore, and my faith is stronger for it."

After the loss of a child, many parents find that their faith takes a direct hit. They cannot believe in a God who would *take* their baby away from them. After all, everyone has told them that this was a part of God's good plan. If this is the case, why would He intentionally cause us such hurt?

Gina has experienced three losses: one at eighteen weeks, one at eight weeks, and one at nineteen weeks. During her first loss, Gina says that she embraced her grief and learned from it; she loved her husband deeper, cherished her children more, and ultimately was grateful for the time she'd been given with her baby. But by her third loss, Gina felt furious with God for not answering prayers to let her keep her baby. She says, "After my last loss, I was in a very dark place. I didn't try to embrace my grief; I ran from it. I was so extremely devastated, I just put on a fake smile for my kids so I could function." Gina felt especially hurt by remarks made from those around her, people who told her that God had "taken the baby from her because He knew she wasn't able to handle whatever was wrong with the child."

The sad reality is that people make these kinds of remarks all the time. Friends or acquaintances may try to comfort you with the fact that "God took your baby home because He 'needed them' more than you did," but this statement is neither true nor biblical. God does not *take* our children away from us. He is not a God who delights in death—quite the opposite, in fact. He came to earth to *defeat* it. He does not find pleasure in seeing us broken-hearted and crushed. The separation that we experience from loved ones is a direct result of living in a fallen and sin-filled world.

We live in a broken world, and there is no denying it. You only have to flick on your TV or scroll through your Facebook newsfeed to see how God's creation has been shattered and smeared by sin. From the very beginning, God designed us to be in relationship. His desire was that we would walk with Him and with one another. But when Adam and Eve bit into that forbidden fruit, and sin burst its way into the world, our punishment was death. For generations, we have wrestled with questions of God's goodness and cried out for understanding. We cannot see the fullness of God's plan, and without sight, we begin to doubt.

But there are truths that we can cling to: the truth of a gracious and loving Father who sent His son to die a horrific death on a wooden cross. With His nail-pierced skin, Jesus defeated death itself that we may be reunited with the God who knit us together in our mother's womb.[12] As followers of Christ, we hold fast to the promise of a great heavenly reunion. Death no longer holds victory over us.[13] In our children's death, they have been ushered into His presence, a place of great rejoicing and unstained joy.[14] We believe in the hope of life eternal, of an eternity spent in worship and glorification of the living God.

Scripture says that the afflictions we face today are "light" and "momentary." This doesn't trivialize the depths of pain you're feeling right now. Quite the contrary! In 2 Corinthians 4:16–17, Paul says, *"So we do not lose heart. Though our outer self is wasting away, our inner self is being renewed day by day. For this light momentary affliction is preparing for us an eternal weight of glory beyond all comparison."* If the depths and duration of the pain we are feeling right now can be called "light and momentary," imagine still how much

---

12 Psalm 139:13.

13 1 Corinthians 15:55.

14 Isaiah 65:17-20.

greater the eternity we long for *must be*. If this—*even this!*—could be called "light," imagine the fullness of reward that awaits the faithful. Our minds cannot comprehend all that is still in store for those who trust in and call upon His name. The sufferings that we face today are but road signs pointing us to the eternal glory of God, preparing us for that which is still to come.

But even though our head may know these scriptural truths, it's not always easy to arrive at the place where we can say, "God is good, even though I am currently separated from my child." The question "why?" may seem insurmountable, looming in front of you and blocking all other light. It can be incredibly difficult to lay your empty, aching body before God and give Him glory in the midst of such uncertainty.

Even though Gina was so incredibly angry after her third loss, she felt a release when she began to honestly lay her feelings and emotions before the Lord. "I didn't hold anything back from God. I attended Adoration at my Catholic Church, journaled, and found beauty amidst nature and horseback riding. I focused on the good and always tried to choose joy, no matter how difficult some days were."

While we flounder along here on earth, we may never find a truly soul-satisfying answer to the question "why?" Sometimes the best we can do is to drag our bruised and bloodied selves to the foot of the cross, draw near to God, and trust that even in this situation, even in our deepest most unfathomable pain, He is here with us, and He is still good. Chances are that you won't get to this understanding overnight. It's a lifelong lesson, one that we tend to have to learn over and over again. Raising our empty hands in submission, offering nothing but ourselves, we can come before Him and say, "God, I don't understand *why* this happened, but I trust you anyway."

Trust. For such a tiny word, it seems awfully hard to grasp. This act of submission is a *daily* response to the struggles, temptations, and worry that we encounter. Our anxiety is quick to rise in stressful situations, our anger or fears quick to rear in moments of uncertainty. And yet through it all we are called to trust: to *daily* and *consciously* place the *whole* of our lives in the hands of God.

I'm reminded of the story of the Israelites in the wilderness. In Exodus 16, we find the Israelites escaped from Egypt. They have seen the might and the power and the wonder of God. And now we find them in the wilderness, hungry. They're grumbling and scared, worried that they're going to die—so much so that they wish God had never rescued them from the Egyptians. They would rather have died in slavery with full bellies. Their physical hunger blinded them to the realities of God, causing them to turn inwards rather than to look to the sustainer and giver of life. They didn't come to God in faith and reliance, remembering His miraculous works of the past. They sat in their tents grumbling. And *still* God heard them. *Still* He was faithful to those whom He had brought out of slavery.

God provided manna for them to eat. From the dew of the morning, white flakes lined the ground of the wilderness—enough for the Israelites to fill themselves. But more than just physical nourishment, God was calling them to trust *daily* in His provision. He did not allow them to store the manna (those that did found it rotting and stinking the next morning) but to go out *each* morning to collect food and to fall asleep *each* night trusting that God would provide for the following day. God gave the Israelites this manna every day for forty years! Four decades of daily trusting that God would provide bread for their children's bellies and that God would keep them from starving in a land far from home.

We too are asked to walk daily in trust with Him. We might not have enough faith today to believe in forty years of manna, but what if we started by just trusting God enough for today? What if we walk through one of the most difficult moments of our lives believing that He will yet again provide for *today*? And then, what if we wake up tomorrow morning, and the next, each time trusting Him for just one more day? We can do this one step at a time. God doesn't expect us to start off running when we haven't yet learned to walk. He knows that our earthly vision is limited and that we're quick to avert our eyes from the solution and instead fixate on the problem. Knowing us more intimately that we could ever even know ourselves, He simply asks us to trust Him with what He has given us: to trust Him for enough manna for today.

Some days it feels near impossible to give up that control and trust that God sees a much bigger picture than we do. It's hard to find peace with our limited knowledge and to find contentment when what we really long for is concrete, tangible answers. After all, what can be more difficult than trusting Him with our children's lives—even to the point of death? But this is what He asks us to do: to trust in Him in all things and to walk fully in His ways. And in return, He promises that no matter what tomorrow brings, He will remain with us: *"Trust in him at all times, O people; pour out your heart before him; God is a refuge for us"* (Psalm 62:8).

Rose, whom we met earlier in this chapter, struggled for a long time with these feelings of anger. She says, "I cursed and questioned God for three years. I just couldn't understand why He would allow me, someone who adores children and has dreamt of motherhood my whole life, to lose my child. When I learned I was pregnant, it brought me back to God ... but when I lost the baby, I ran away again. Thankfully, after three long years, I am back to seeking God and working to restore the faith that I used to hold so dear to my heart. I have a renewed desire to draw near to Him, and I'm thankful to Him for showing me what I could have missed had I held on to this anger and pain."

It's okay to be angry with God. It's okay to have questions. He knows the burdens of your heart and the deep-rooted emotions that soak your pillow each night and scream out in agony. You cannot hide these emotions from Him,[15] so let Him help carry them instead. Trusting God doesn't mean that our pain and grief will dissipate overnight. Admitting that we're angry and wounded isn't some magic formula that promises to put everything "back to the way it was before." But God does promise to meet you *here*. Surrounded by the mess and sting of our heartache, cry out to Him! You don't have to do this apart from Him. You don't have to grieve on your own. God is strong enough to carry your wounds. In the middle of your anger and finger-pointing, take a deep breath and place this hurt and pain in His hands.

Let go, and see what He does.

> *The Lord is a stronghold for the oppressed, a stronghold in times of trouble. And those who know your name put their trust in you, for you, O Lord, have not forsaken those who seek you.*
>
> —Psalm 9:9–10

---

15 Psalm 139:7.

Journaling Prompts

What Do We Do with Our Anger and Guilt?

- Out of the four categories we've discussed, which ones (if any) do you feel you fit into? Why do you think that you find blame in these specific areas? How do you think this blame will affect your grieving process long term?

- Write down some practical ways that you can begin letting go of these feelings of guilt and blame. Are you ready to let go? It's important to wrestle with difficult issues and not simply pass them over. In your journaling, try to dig deep and uncover *why* you feel the need to carry this guilt, blame, or anger. Is it a control issue? A pain issue? Something else?

- After the loss of a child, your faith can take a beating and be either strengthened or bloodied by this death. What do you feel towards God right now? Have your feelings changed over the course of your grief?

Chapter Five
Dealing with Triggers

It was Easter Sunday, and although we were a few minutes early, the church building was already feeling crowded. We were in the process of looking for a new home church, and this was our first visit to the large, downtown congregation. College-aged kids in ripped jeans, elderly men with polished shoes, and little girls in fancy, floral dresses all squeezed their way into the theatre-turned-sanctuary to celebrate and remember the work of the cross. It felt good to gather together.

The main floor was quickly filling and, with our son in his arms, my husband made a beeline for the signs marked "family seating." The crowd forced us a few steps apart as I grimly determined not to knock over any Easter-hatted ladies with my ridiculously oversized diaper bag. Catching up with my husband, I stopped short when I saw who was seated in the row immediately in front of us.

Two matching car seats perched casually on the velvet-covered pew while teeny babies swaddled in hipster blankets and knit caps slept peacefully inside: *newborn twins*. My breath caught in my throat and I felt as if I'd been punched in the stomach. I'd yet to see my hopes and dreams laid out so clearly before my eyes, but here they were, dozing quietly, reminding me of everything I'd never have. The babies were obviously preemies, and it felt entirely plausible that the mother had decided to swing by the church service on her way home from the hospital. A crowd of excited well-wishers were already gathering around to congratulate the new parents. It was obvious that this was the babies' first public appearance.

"I can't do this. I can't sit there."

I wasn't sure if my husband had heard my panicked whisper. But he had. Understanding flooded his face, and we wordlessly made our way towards an open spot on the opposite end of the building. My husband patted my hand knowingly as I pressed a tissue under my eyelids and fought to keep my tears from flowing out.

This sudden burst of raw emotion hit me unexpectedly, and I was left wondering if I'd overreacted. Was I some kind of grief-laden drama queen? I didn't want to be the woman bawling in the middle of the Easter service, the one who was unable to keep it all together. Almost a year into my grief, I'd thought that this piercing passion had been worn down to a gentle ache. Surely I should be finished grieving with this intensity? It wasn't as if I hadn't seen twins before. I'd steeled myself for these encounters, bracing and cautioning myself against the jagged stab of pain that would inevitably come. But nothing prepared me for the sudden rush of grief flowing up over the sight of these two newborn babies.

Psychologists refer to these brief moments as a "sudden, temporary upsurge of grief," a common and healthy part of the grieving process. Just when you think you may be getting a handle on this ever-morphing cloud of emotion, you feel the red-hot sting of yet another welt—a reminder of all the things we are powerless to control.

A few months later, I sat in a coffee shop with another loss mom. Sipping iced tea and munching on banana bread, we cautiously opened our hearts and began discussing the complexity of life after loss. After experiencing a stillbirth, she and her husband had had to take a break from church—it had been too difficult to face the numerous expectant mothers and their tiny newborns every Sunday morning. Her first service back, she'd left in tears.

Upon hearing her confession, I exhaled a breath that I didn't even know I'd been holding. I was so relieved to know that someone else had dealt with these triggers. I wasn't over-exaggerating this pain. I wasn't alone in these emotions and feelings.

While these triggers come in all shapes and sizes, grieving mothers often find themselves triggered by the sight of another woman's healthy pregnancy or her newborn baby. In the immediate aftermath of loss, some women stop attending baby showers—they simply can't bear to be surrounded by infant gear and chocolate-smeared diaper games. Other times, friends' pregnancy announcements or newborn photoshoot pictures can cause sudden flashbacks or unexpected memories. Loss mama Christy says, "I'm triggered by people close to me becoming pregnant, people being pregnant with girls, and people close to me delivering their babies. Random people don't bother me as much now (it did in the beginning), but watching my friends experience what I didn't get to is still really hard."

Another common trigger is meeting children who share the same name as your lost baby. Julie shares how just hearing the names of her babies makes her sad: "One baby we named 'Jubilee,' and later in church we were singing a contemporary version of the hymn, 'Be Thou My Vision.' One of the lines, instead of saying, 'May I reach Heaven's joys' actually said 'May I see Heaven's jubilee …' I totally lost it. I broke down crying, thinking of my sweet Jubilee who is in Heaven. My husband got tears in his eyes and gave me a great big hug. He knew exactly what had triggered me."

In the early stages of grief, these deep, painful responses may be much more frequent and acute, but they can also pop up randomly for months or years afterwards. While we may choose to try and avoid these situations altogether, it's impossible to escape every trigger. Even if we locked ourselves in our apartments for the rest of our lives (not a particularly healthy option), we'd still face the constant barrage of triggers found in social media, books, music, TV, or seemingly random household items. Grief doesn't always make sense—when it comes to triggers, there is no "one size fits all." Sarah, for example, finds herself in tears over peanut butter. "It sounds silly," she says, "but I couldn't buy peanut butter at the store for months after our second loss. For the nine weeks I'd been pregnant, it was the only thing I could eat on toast in the morning that I wouldn't instantly throw back up."

We all know that it can be embarrassing to find yourself suddenly overcome with grief (especially if these triggers occur abruptly in a public place), but it's important to understand that healthy grief takes time. Today the pain may feel all-consuming, but with the passage of time comes gentle release. You may be wading sluggishly through life, trying to get through it minute by minute or hour by hour, but eventually that grief will stretch out into day by day, week by week. The grief gets a little easier to carry, but that doesn't mean it disappears completely, or that your child has been forgotten.

The fear of a child being forgotten is a common source of anxiety for many loss mothers—it was certainly one of mine. These little ones had such an impact on my life, and it was scary to begin moving forward without them. Over the passing months, the intensity of my grief began to slowly evolve into a dull ache. I was afraid to let go of the sharp sting of pain; my tears were a reminder of my love, and I felt guilty for the days I didn't cry. I worried that as I began to heal, I would begin to forget.

In some ways, these temporary surges of grief are refreshing. Even years down the road, it serves as a physical reassurance that we haven't forgotten our children and that we still carry their memories with me. My dear friend Rhonda miscarried a baby over seven years ago, yet she says that these triggers still come out of the blue and surprise her.

Rhonda's Story

It was Rhonda's third pregnancy. All seemed normal until her twelve-week ultrasound failed to show a heartbeat. While the doctor was unconcerned, Rhonda expressed her fears, so her doctor booked another appointment for the fourteen-week mark. Two weeks later, while out for a run, Rhonda began to spot. After heading to the hospital and explaining her symptoms and history, they booked her in for an ultrasound the next morning.

The next morning's ultrasound showed a baby who was only ten weeks in size, and the technicians questioned whether Rhonda's dates could be correct. Sending her to her family doctor, the doctor said she believed Rhonda was experiencing a "missed abortion." She explained that the fetus had most likely died, but Rhonda's body had continued with the pregnancy as normal for the next four weeks. By this time, the cramps and bleeding confirmed what was happening.

After receiving a prescription for pills to help force out the miscarried fetus, Rhonda prayed about what to do. That evening, with a heavy heart, she took the first dose of pills and sent her children and husband to bed. Within an hour the cramps started, and by the time she was scheduled to take her second dose of pills, she was in considerable pain. "By the time two and a half hours had passed, I was in severe pain, equivalent to labour. I was praying, because I didn't know how much more of it I could take. Suddenly I felt a small pop and a huge gush. I ran to the bathroom but didn't get there in time. I hardly knew what to do, there was so much blood."

Over the course of the next day, Rhonda continued to bleed profusely and headed back to the hospital for the third day in a row. The gynecologist there told her that the "products of conception had not come out and were sitting on her uterus." He would have to "manually extract them," which most women find "a bit uncomfortable." Rhonda was so exhausted, emotionally spent, and physically traumatized that she just lay there, quietly letting the tears roll out of her eyes.

"The doctor worked a bit more and then said, 'You know what? I'm going to finish this in the OR. You'll go to sleep and when you wake up, it'll be done.' I was so thankful for that bit of grace. On his way out, he put the pan with the contents of our labour of love on the counter and asked if we'd like to see it. I declined, but to this day I regret that, as it was the only opportunity to see our baby, who was not a baby or a person to anyone but us. Later, after the procedure, I woke up and felt relieved that it was finally over."

Rhonda says that what has surprised her about the loss is all the random times she remembers this little baby and what might have been. "These reminders of what I never got occur suddenly and stir up emotions even years later. I couldn't believe that something so small could cause such a great hurt." Rhonda says that the physical experience of the event itself was traumatic, which made it more challenging to grieve. "The carpet from our living room to the hallway was stained by the profusion of blood and was a constant reminder. My husband finally cut that section out and patch-worked the hallway back together with some leftover carpet. Even though it looked terrible to visitors with all the seams and mismatched patterns, I finally had some freedom from the visual reminder of that terrible night and day."

Rhonda's story is just another painful but precious reminder of the fact that for the rest of our lives, we will carry this small, baby-sized scar. In the months or years to come, this scar may suddenly or unexpectedly flare up, *and that's okay*. If we live long enough and love hard enough, we will all eventually encounter the difficult task of learning to grieve. It shouldn't be seen as a weakness, something to be embarrassed by or quickly overcome, but rather as a reminder that we loved. To see our grief as a declaration of love is to glimpse beauty amidst the sorrow.

But it's not always easy to look at our grief and embrace it as something beautiful or beneficial. It hurts too much. How can we learn to grow in faith in the middle of such despair? How can we begin to see grief as something good, rather than just pain? Where can we experience the confidence and freedom to fully grieve?

Katherine is a mom who not only understands the triggers that come with life after loss but has also embraced great hope throughout her grief. After miscarrying a baby at six weeks, Katherine was met soon afterwards with the arrival of her newborn niece. "Hearing my husband's siblings talk about their impending birth was so hard for me. We were very close with them and had journeyed with them through the pregnancy, but now I wanted to avoid any talk of babies. For a time, I didn't want to even see my sister-in-law's pregnant belly." Katherine, however, was unwilling to let these feelings take root in her life, and she says that God was gracious to help her walk through these emotions. "I felt my soul crave the encouragement of scripture to bring life to my bones and prayer to lift my spirits. When I prayed about my feelings of envy, God allowed me to enter into the space where I could truly rejoice with my brother and sister-in-law and support them after the birth."

Like Katherine, we too can learn to embrace and explore our grief through the scriptures. In a time of loss, one of the most comforting and instructing places to turn to is the book of Psalms.

Some of the most powerful psalms were written in a time of deep anguish. They show us the depth of human despondency and point us to a God who is still worthy of our time, our praise, and our love. Even for those of us who have grown up reading the psalms, re-reading these chapters through the lens of loss can bring a whole new level of understanding to many of the passages.

As you reflect on your own understanding of grief, take a few moments to read through the following psalm. When reading it, feel free to highlight or underline any lines that seem particularly applicable to your grief journey thus far.

As the deer pants for streams of water, so my soul pants for you, my God. My soul thirsts for God, for the living God. When can I go and meet with God? My tears have been my food day and night, while people say to me all day long, "Where is your God?" These things I remember as I pour out my soul: how I used to go to the house of God under the protection of the Mighty One with shouts of joy and praise among the festive throng. Why, my soul, are you downcast? Why so disturbed within me? Put your hope in God, for I will yet praise him, my Savior and my God. My soul is downcast within me; therefore I will remember you from the land of the Jordan, the heights of Hermon—from Mount Mizar. Deep calls to deep in the roar of your waterfalls; all your waves and breakers have swept over me. By day the L<small>ORD</small> *directs his love, at night his song is with me— a prayer to the God of my life. I say to God my Rock, "Why have you forgotten me? Why must I go about mourning, oppressed by the enemy?" My bones suffer mortal agony as my foes taunt me, saying to me all day long, "Where is your God?" Why, my soul, are you downcast? Why so disturbed within me? Put your hope in God, for I will yet praise him, my Savior and my God.*

—Psalm 42:1–11 (NIV)

This psalm is a really great example of what it means to embrace our grief. The lament doesn't avoid sorrow but faces it head-on. In the midst of deep, unrelenting pain, the author fights to hold on to hope and continually seeks a deeper understanding of God. Even in the midst of depression, he leans into his pain and uses it as an opportunity to not only reflect on God's faithfulness and love but to *praise* Him! This is what our grief should drive us to do.

Oftentimes, particularly when we're hurting, we approach the scriptures with a very me-centric attitude. We look for what we can get out of it and pick verses based on what comfort we can find. But the scriptures are more than just soft, fuzzy encouragement or empty poetic words. They provide solace for an aching soul, primarily because they show us *who* God is. As we study and learn about God's character, we gain a better understanding of the world around us (a world that He has designed, structured, and ordered) and are reminded to pursue the creator rather than the created. You may feel lower than you have ever been before, but this grief *can* push you to new heights with the God who is worthy of all our worship.

Over and over again, I have encountered countless women who have felt their faith stretched and tested but ultimately strengthened by this heartbreaking journey. It's not easy and it's not immediate, but this grief is not without hope. Soak in the scriptures daily and allow them to minister to your wounds. God's Word offers peace and hope without denying or using Band-Aids to mask our grief. Our heavenly Father understands our pain; He knows the triggers we face, and in response, He simply asks us to draw closer to Him.

From the lips of women who have just walked through the worst experience of their lives comes testament to the exponential growth of faith in times of hardship. One of those women was Christy, a mother who knows what it's like to walk through fire and emerge refined on the other side. "It's been a difficult place to get to, but now I am *so* much closer to Jesus than I ever was in the past. I know that without my suffering, my faith wouldn't be where it is today."

Another mama, Lexi, says, "Scripture says that God works *all* things to His purposes. Nothing happened outside of the will of God. My pregnancy loss was and still is used by God to this day for my good and ultimately His glory. I may never understand how or why that is true, but God's Word can be trusted, no matter what the world around me says. God is good all the time."

These are but two examples amidst a sea of fellow sisters in Christ. Grief may feel overwhelming right now. It may be difficult to face constant trigger after trigger, but know that there *is* comfort, strength, and hope to be found. As you encounter the triggers hidden in the world around you, give opportunity for your sorrow to pull you into closer relationship with God. As you reflect and journal through the questions in this chapter, pull out your Bible, flip through to Psalms, and let the healing words minister to your aching soul.

He is here with you today. Cry out to Him.

Save me, O God! For the waters have come up to my neck. I sink in deep mire, where there is no foothold; I have come into deep waters, and the flood sweeps over me. I am weary with my crying out; my throat is parched. My eyes grow dim with waiting for my God.
—Psalm 69:1–3

Before concluding this chapter, it's important to note that these triggers and intense bouts of emotion are usually momentary and manageable. If they're accompanied by feelings of self-harm or emotions that are too overwhelming to handle, they may be a sign of something more serious at work. Katie shares one such example: "My sister-in-law had a son that was due two weeks after my twin girls. When I went to the hospital to visit him, it triggered such an intense panic attack that I wanted to throw myself out the hospital window." After the death of her daughters, Katie struggled with postpartum depression and severe anxiety. While these triggers are normally a healthy part of grief, be sure to talk with a medical professional if you find yourself struggling and unable to cope with the emotions and desires that arise. There is never any shame in seeking help or in admitting that you can't do this on your own.

Journaling Prompts
What Are Your Triggers?

- "Knowing your triggers" is an important part of figuring out how you will respond to them. What are some triggers that you face on a day to day basis? How do you deal with them?

- Read through Psalms 31 and 34. What does the Bible teach us about grieving and how to grieve? Are there any verses that stand out to you in these passages? Spend some time contemplating and journaling through these psalms.

- On your darkest days, do you feel nearer to or farther from God? How has the good news of Christ and the truths found in scripture helped you to walk through this time of grief? In your journal, write out a prayer to God, asking Him to draw near to you. List instances of God's past faithfulness over your life. Re-read this prayer aloud on days when you feel alone.

Chapter Six
Comparing

I pressed my fingers up against the warm glass of his incubator and watched my newborn's chest rise and fall softly in sleep. Like most other days this month, I'd spent the past eight hours huddled in a chair in the neonatal unit waiting for those brief moments when my son would awake and I could hold him. I pumped breastmilk by his bedside, and after handing it off to a nurse, I whispered my good-byes. With one son in the NICU and the other buried in a cemetery, I was headed home for yet another night without my babies.

Making my way to an empty bench outside the hospital, I waited for my husband to finish work and pick me up. The past month had left me feeling emotionally bruised, and I savoured these few minutes in the fresh air, soaking up the warmth of stray summer rays. It didn't help the sharp, stabbing pain in my chest, but it didn't hurt either. For the next twenty minutes, I sat and watched as waddling pregnant women and smiling visitors with balloons hurried in and out of the glass hospital doors. Most of them looked right past me. With my saggy tummy and tired, watery eyes, there wasn't much to hold their attention.

A father jumped out of a car parked at the curb and began to carefully load his slow-moving wife and newborn baby into the backseat. They were going home. With every step, the beaming parents radiated a wave of pride, nerves, and pure delight. Caught up in a world of wonder, they smiled broadly in my direction and offered up a silent invitation for me to join them in this brief moment of bliss. I desperately wished to share in their excitement, to feel something, but I couldn't seem to get further than the fake smile twisted on my face. This may have been their happiest day, but it certainly wasn't mine.

I watched as the family carefully strapped their baby into the car and tried desperately to ignore the rising lump of pain emanating from my gut. I'd already come to recognize this all-too-familiar feeling, the bitter twinge of jealousy leaving a bad taste in my mouth.

Envy: for a four-letter word, it can sure pack a huge amount of oomph. We see the dreams of others fulfilled while ours lay crumbling into dust at our feet, and we wonder why we don't have what they do. The jealousy crosses unbidden to mind, the ache of one who dreams of days when we were lighter and free from pain. The sight of a newborn baby or a pregnant mama sparks a longing deep within us: remembrances of days when life was comparatively carefree. When your arms are empty, it's so easy to begin envying those whose wombs gave way to squalling, healthy, full-term babies. It's easy to envy those who seemingly have it all.

Fellow loss mom Joy admits that she has felt these feelings often: "I feel jealous of other pregnant women," Joy shares. "Sometimes I wonder why these mothers get to keep their baby, and I didn't. It makes me mad. And then I just feel bad, because I wouldn't actually wish this kind of loss on anyone. It's a rollercoaster of emotion all the time."

We know that these thoughts aren't ones of grace or justice for the other mamas, but these rising feelings of "unfairness" still linger. Why does one mother get to keep what the other does not? Fellow grieving mom Lindsey speaks with incredible honesty as she says, "Seeing a pregnant woman triggers my grief. I'm always amazed and so envious that some women get to experience a big pregnant belly or flutters inside. I feel a twinge of anger when I see a pregnant woman. I don't believe she appreciates just how lucky she really is. It's a horrible thought to have about someone, I know, but it's how I feel nonetheless."

Pregnancy loss is never a pretty experience. It can feel ugly and dark to look upon the raw, painful emotions buried deep within us—things that we might not otherwise think or say. But by sharing our stories with honesty and vulnerability, we cast light into an otherwise broken situation. We show women that we're not alone in these feelings and that we're not a "bad person" for letting our grief erupt in the way that it does. As difficult as it may be to put into practice, we should not let our fear shame us from sharing the inconvenient and uncomfortable truths of pregnancy loss.

Lindsey's Story

This honesty and courage are what I find so remarkable about Lindsey's story. When Lindsey was nineteen weeks pregnant with her third child, she began to spot. Sitting in the doctor's office waiting for an ultrasound machine, Lindsey wondered if her life was about to change.

"The doctor pulled up the baby on the screen and didn't say anything for a full minute. I knew then that I had lost my little one. He measured sixteen weeks gestational age, which meant that I had carried him for three weeks without a heartbeat. I called my mom, who was watching my two older children, and I broke down in tears. I don't remember much of that night. We took our kids to the local beer shop and I downed two beers. Someone came over with a bottle of wine and I drank the majority of that too. I spoke to my dad and we both cried. My kids put on clown noses and made me laugh (albeit half-hearted laughter), and then that evening I cried myself to sleep."

The next morning, Lindsey's cramps turned into contractions that were five minutes apart. "I told my husband that we needed to go to the emergency room, because there was no way I was going to birth a dead baby in my bathroom. I checked into the ER, and a nurse who reminded me of Santa Claus helped me get comfortable. The nurse gave me a sedative, the on-call doctor spoke with me, the accounts receivable man took my credit card to process the co-pay, and then I was alone." Physically alone in the room, Lindsey felt something slip out of her and knew that she had just given birth. There was no pain, no discomfort, just tears and the feeling of being in a surreal nightmare. Pressing her call button for assistance, the doctor confirmed that she had given birth to a baby boy.

"My baby was wrapped in a bedsheet and placed on the television stand at the front of the room. I couldn't decide whether I should keep staring at the bundle or avoid eye contact with it. My husband and I were told that we would need to decide whether or not we were going to look at the baby. We ultimately decided not to. I knew that the baby would not look like what a baby should, and I did not want that image of my son burned into memory."

Instead, Lindsey had an autopsy technician take hand and footprints, a memory which she treasures. "Looking back on the whole experience, there were a lot of things that went right: I didn't birth the baby at home, I didn't have any discomfort, my recovery was immediate, and my other two children never knew about the pregnancy and therefore didn't have to grieve like we did. I held on to these positives for dear life, willing them to take away the sting of losing my baby."

Lindsey goes on to say, "A few days after my first miscarriage, I saw a social media post from a pregnant friend who had just heard her baby's heartbeat. I shouldn't have been offended by this, but the pictures stung, especially since she was aware of my situation. This is a trait and an experience that makes me feel ashamed and very self-involved. It's not something that I'm proud of. My emotional recovery with this loss was slow. I cried a lot and I drank a lot. I pretended that I was fine when really, I probably wasn't."

Lindsey went on to have two additional miscarriages after that, one at thirteen weeks and one at five. "Miscarriage changes a person tremendously," Lindsey says. "It fills you with anxiety, fear, longing, heartache, and guilt—basically every emotion possible. I wish that I didn't have to experience all of this. I look at other pregnant women and make harsh judgements without even knowing them as people. It's a trait that I don't like, and I think it stems from my pregnancy losses. I have no clue what these women have gone through or what their stories are, but for some reason, I envy them and wish that they could feel what I feel, just for a minute."

If we're honest, we too have probably found ourselves (at some point or another) judging other mothers. We watch their stories unfold and we ache over the fact that ours seems so incomplete in comparison. As soon as those pink lines first appear on a pregnancy test, you begin to build a mental image of the emotions that accompany motherhood: the protective, blissful feelings that come with nurturing and raising a child. We dream of quiet afternoons spent breastfeeding and bonding, and powerful mom-kisses that wipe away all tears. Now when we look at social media posts of tired but smiling mothers and their contentedly sleeping newborns, we grieve the motherhood we'd dreamed of. We mourn the future we never had.

Newly grieving mother Kelly shares the words that so many of us have felt after loss: "I feel robbed of getting to experience our baby's heartbeat, feeling their first kicks, or the joy of holding them for the first time. I missed seeing them smile, roll over, sit up, and their first steps."

Kelly was almost nine weeks pregnant when she lost the baby that her husband and she had fought so hard for. After four-plus years of fertility issues and medications, IUIs, laparoscopy surgeries, and a diagnosis of endometriosis, Kelly discovered that she was pregnant. When their second ultrasound revealed no heartbeat, her doctor scheduled her for a D&C the next morning. Two weeks later, it was discovered that Kelly has a blood clotting disorder called MTHFR, or methylenetetrahydrofolate reductase (something that they wouldn't have known without the miscarriage).

Kelly adds, "Grief is a natural process, and if we don't address it, it will run wild. I was robbed of the joy that comes with experiencing my baby's firsts, and that's difficult to process. But ultimately, I celebrate the fact that my baby was here. Sometimes life isn't what we expected. That doesn't mean that we won't be able to find joy again—it just means that it may take us on a different path than what we'd anticipated."

If you're reading this book, it's likely that your motherhood journey is vastly different than what you'd imagined it would be. I too had spent seven months of pregnancy imagining what those initial moments of motherhood look like. I eagerly anticipated the feelings of relief and utter joy as the doctors laid two, squirming babies against my chest. I could picture the first family photo as my husband and I, with tears in our eyes, proudly held our precious babies in our arms and nuzzled the peach fuzz atop their tiny little heads. These dreams were left unfulfilled, another loss to be mourned. Amidst the blur of hospital visits and casket choices, I struggled to *feel* the way that I thought a new mother *should* feel. As I watched the new mothers in the maternity ward around me, I glimpsed a world of happiness that I felt unable to participate in. Instead of the motherhood I'd expected, my first moments with my sons were marred by acrid sorrow and intense grief. I felt robbed of my "motherhood firsts," and worse yet, I felt guilty. Envious of the other moms' all-encompassing happiness, I felt miserable for being unable to resurrect that same surge of joyous emotion for my surviving twin. Overwhelmed by a torrent of grief, and exhausted by the energy it took to get through each day, I mostly just felt numb.

The entirety of this emotion was encapsulated for me a few days after my first loss. As my husband and I drove home from a funeral appointment, I watched a smiling mother push her stroller along the sidewalk. She appeared to be carefree as she laughed and tucked a loose blanket around her little one; the sun was shining, and her smile was broad. In the moment it took me to drive past her, I thought to myself that it wasn't fair. I wanted to be that mom. I wanted to go back to the time when I'd never felt such heavy sorrow corroding my joy, and I worried that I would *never* be able to feel wholly happy again. Would my laughter forever remain a hollow imitation of what it was before?

My innocence had shattered, and I was left holding bits of pieces that would never fit back together. I ached for not only the baby I'd lost but for myself as well—for the woman I thought I'd lost on that fated delivery day.

Perhaps you've felt the same: that desire to go back to the time *before*. Back to the day before the loss or the diagnosis, back to the time when things hurt less and when happiness didn't feel so far away. A dividing line has been drawn in the sand, and, truthfully, while the pain may lessen, there *are* some things that have been lost forever. Our understanding of pregnancy's fragility has blossomed overnight, but with that arrives an ever-increased sense of anxiety and helplessness. As our baby slips from our womb, so does the light-hearted naivety we once held.

"My loss was my first pregnancy," shares Emily, "so I feel somewhat robbed of the ability to ever enjoy a pregnancy. Everyone else I know who is pregnant is so excited, posting little updates on Facebook, painting nurseries, and I'm just waiting in a sort of stasis, too scared to bond with my new baby or buy anything for him in case he dies. I'm often jealous of other women's innocence."

When our own bellies feel so woefully flat and flabby, the round bellies of the pregnant women at church or the mall seem to taunt us. While we know that our own loss should not prevent us from feeling happy for others, it hurts to see someone else so successful at something we feel we've failed at. After my miscarriages, I envied these mamas' stretch-marks and swollen ankles, their freedom from fear, and their beautiful birth stories. Every pregnant woman who crossed my path was another reminder of the life I no longer carried.

Tara-Lynn echoes a similar sentiment. "After my miscarriage, I would become quite jealous and incapable of feeling joy for those who were expecting. I remember going to a baby shower and crying my way through it. I looked at people who got pregnant unexpectedly or out of wedlock, and I'd feel as if it wasn't fair. Even though I now have one living child, I still battle with some of these feelings when I feel that the person isn't deserving of pregnancy or such a happy ending."

In today's world of social media, our definition of "motherhood" has gotten a little twisted. We choose to share photos that make ourselves feel good, pictures where we feel glamorous, pretty, or happy. We paint a portrait of life that's altogether different from our day to day reality. Looking at friends' and acquaintances' lives from the outside, we could naturally begin to assume that they have it all together. We see vacation pics, date nights, smiles, baby cuddles, and five-star desserts. We don't see real life. We don't see a floor littered with carrot muffin crumbs and Legos, that bottle of milk spilling onto the carpet, and that two-day-old dirty diaper stinking up the bathroom. We don't see their tears of frustration and exhaustion, the days full of laundry and dishes, takeout food, and daycare pickups.

As much as we envy the lives of the pregnant women around us, it's easy to forget that we don't have the whole story. Our expectations for motherhood have been erroneously based on a collection of highly edited and posed Facebook photos. We see modern motherhood through Instagram filters and funny Twitter updates, maternity shoots, and gossipy magazine articles. And when we fail to live up to these impossibly high standards, when we feel as if we're missing out on the motherhood that *everyone else* has, we defeat ourselves. We listen to lies, not truth. We compare real life to one-sided pictures that only serve to stir up unfounded feelings of inadequacy, envy, and guilt. As much as celebrities would like to have us imagine otherwise, the snapshots of hospital-gowned mothers and their sleeping newborns don't tell the whole story.

Many of the women we've been envying have their own tales of grief and heartache—we just don't get the chance to see it very often. Rarely do we post photos that show the pain of infertility, postpartum depression, miscarriage, stillbirth, gestational diabetes, life-threatening illness, children with disabilities, and pregnancies lived in fear. For many women, *this* is what real motherhood looks like.

In a time when community is most important, we may accidentally isolate ourselves from those who could offer support. We're so busy envying mothers of their "perfect" after-labour photos to see that behind their toothy grins are women whose journeys are just as colourful, messy, and imperfect as ours. Real life is never perfect—and that's okay. It's okay to have an imperfect story. It's okay to not feel the way you're "supposed" to feel. It's okay to feel nothing. It's okay to curl up in a tightly wound ball and cry until there are no more tears. It's okay to be angry, exhausted, or confused. And when the day comes that you begin feeling happy again, that's okay too. There's no guilt in laughter.

As we struggle to stop comparing and simply embrace, we begin to be satisfied with the story that we've been given—a story that is complete in all its imperfections, a story that does not look like our friends' Facebook accounts but is beautiful in its own right. And in this place of mourning, sitting empty and numb, and desperately wishing to feel "normal" again, it's important to remember that there is a God who is stronger. There is One whose grace is sufficient and whose power is made perfect in weakness. There is a healing Father who can use this broken story for His glory. There is a God who brings joy to a weary heart.

Your life and your story can be used as a testimony of God's goodness. God doesn't ask us to compare our pain or triumphs to that of anyone else. He simply asks that we turn our eyes to Him and Him alone. Forget about comparisons. Don't focus on what He's teaching your friends or neighbours. What is He teaching *you* in this moment?

> *In all this you greatly rejoice, though now for a little while you may have had to suffer grief in all kinds of trials. These have come so that the proven genuineness of your faith—of greater worth than gold, which perishes even though refined by fire—may result in praise, glory and honor when Jesus Christ is revealed.*
>
> —1 Peter 1:6–7, NIV

Journaling Prompts

Who Do You Compare Yourself To?

- What kind of "motherhood firsts" do you feel robbed of? What did you dream that motherhood would look like?

- Do you ever feel envious of other mothers' stories? Why do you think you've been given the story you have? Would you change it if you could? Why or why not?

- When you think of the word "motherhood," what comes to mind? How has society misconstrued this definition? You may not have a baby in your arms, but you are still a mother. What do you wish people knew about your motherhood story?

Chapter Seven

Supporting a Grieving Spouse

"How's your wife doing?" This question seems to hover around your husband lately. With a concerned pat on the arm, your friends and family members, sympathetic co-workers, and church ladies with casseroles, all quietly approach your spouse to ask about your wellbeing. Your husband answers their questions about "how they can help" and says a few polite words. He's been acting as your buffer lately, your protector against an onslaught of well-meaning but overwhelming questions. He tries to shield you from further pain, to wrap you up in his arms and erase your tears. He likes to fix things, to solve problems, but it's hard to repair the wounds of your broken heart. He stands tall and looks strong—as if the grief hasn't touched him—but it has. It just looks different than it does for you or me.

Whether he admits it out loud or not, this grief has settled on a part of him too. Gone are the days when fathers were relegated to the hospital waiting room throughout the delivery, their newspaper and cigars in hand. The role of the father has shifted, and they've become actively involved in the pregnancy, labour, and childrearing processes. Your spouse was there for the ultrasounds and the prenatal classes, he reminded you to take your daily vitamins, and he let you wear his sweatpants when you outgrew your maternity jeans. Your husband sat in the ER with you all night long as the nurses ran bloodwork tests and told you that your blissful few weeks of pregnancy were ending. He walked the hospital hall with you as you laboured, rubbed your back, and fetched you ice chips. And then he watched as the nurse delivered a small infant who never cried but, instead, was cried over.

A mother isn't the only one who mourns her baby. While we naturally pay more attention to the grieving wife, we sometimes forget that the father is hurting too. We see how strong he appears to be, and we forget to ask him, "How are *you* doing?"

Andrea's Story

When Andrea and her husband learned that they were pregnant, the couple went out for a celebratory dinner at an upscale restaurant. Discussing this exciting new stage of their lives, Andrea playfully asked her husband, "What if we have twins?"

Shaking his head, he could only reply, "Don't even say that!" The idea of two was too frightening for him to dwell on.

A few weeks later, they discovered that Andrea *was* pregnant with twins. After the initial shock of that discovery wore off, Andrea felt nothing but elation and an immense longing to one day hold both of her little ones. But at fourteen weeks, they lost one of their babies. Andrea says, "I don't believe that anything could have prepared me for the confusing and contradicting emotions I experienced. I lost one baby but still had to carry a second live baby to birth. I felt an enormous pressure to grieve quickly and 'move on,' because I still had this live baby in my belly that I needed to care for. My husband was there for me as much as he possibly could be, but he was grieving himself and had a completely different perspective on our loss than I did."

After the loss of her child, Andrea couldn't help but think that it had something to do with that night at the restaurant—the moment when her husband had told her not to even mention the possibility of twins. "He was ecstatic when we learned that we were having twins," Andrea says, "but he was also scared, and I blamed him for that fear."

When it came time to deliver her son, everything that could have gone wrong, did. The birth was extremely difficult, and afterwards, the buried grief and the trauma she experienced during labour quickly caught up to her. Immediately, Andrea began experiencing severe postpartum depression. "I lost myself," she says. "After almost two years of this struggle, seriously contemplating suicide, I (with my husband and mother's support) finally checked myself into a full-time outpatient program."

Andrea felt a diminutive amount of support from friends and family after her loss, particularly during her struggle with PPD. Her husband and she decided to give themselves a fresh start to heal and moved from their home state to Southern California, where they found healthier groups with likeminded and positive influences.

While their marriage was ultimately strengthened from this devastating experience, the aftermath of grief and a traumatic birth was difficult on the couple's relationship. Because of his past military deployments, Andrea's husband also experienced severe post-traumatic stress disorder (PTSD) and anxiety. "My husband struggles to handle himself appropriately in emotional situations, because he's been conditioned to detach emotionally," Andrea says. "He wasn't very supportive during my labour or birth. This fueled my postpartum depression and almost caused us to separate. But on the other hand, my husband has gone above and beyond to help me heal and recover from my PPD. He never put himself before me or my son and is an amazing father. We're polar opposites and dealt with our grief in our own ways, but once we began to heal from all the pain, grief, and sorrow that we had experienced, our marriage was made stronger."

Husbands and wives grieve differently—of that there is no doubt—and the way this grief plays out will differ from husband to husband. After asking loss mother Cassie to explain some differences between her husband's and her grief, she said, "It's easy for my husband to not think about our loss and to close that chapter in his mind. While he hasn't forgotten about it, he's able to go day to day without dwelling on it. I almost envy him in that sense, because I'm not able to compartmentalize like that."

This is true for many marriages. In general, men and women express and process their grief through very different methods. For example, the fact that you're reading this book speaks to one of the ways in which you *personally* process your grief. While women may wish to vocalize and discuss their feelings, men often grow up being taught to control rather than display their emotions. These societal pressures also contribute to a husband's desire to remain "strong" for his wife. Being a supportive husband is very much a *good* thing; however, in his desire to be an emotional rock for you, he still needs time and space to process his own grief.

For those who do take time to process this loss, these feelings and emotions may be released in much more concrete, physical outlets—for example, working more or spending time on physical projects or hobbies. There may also be differences in desire for sexual intimacy. One spouse may crave this intimacy as a way to feel close and united, while the other may desire physical closeness but not necessarily sex.

Many grieving mothers have also noted differences in the grief timeline between a husband and a wife. If the baby was lost during early pregnancy, fathers have less concrete memories with their child and may grieve quicker than their partner. My friend Katherine says, "My husband was first and foremost the best support I had during this time of grief. We grieved together, and at times I was a little concerned that he didn't have many people to help support him, as it greatly affected him too. But he was able to move on from the grief a lot faster than I was. He kept encouraging me, praying for me, and redirecting me to the promises of God during this time."

Your husband may not fit into any of the above generalizations, or he may feel that he fits into all of them. The important thing is to acknowledge that your husband *is* grieving, just in his own way. A father's dreams for his child are just as real as a mother's: they dream of the day they would get to walk their daughter down the aisle, or teach their child to ride a bike, throw a baseball, or drive a car. Just like you, they grieve the future they never got.

My husband's first official Father's Day was spent at our summer cabin by the lake. With temperatures soaring into the triple digits Fahrenheit, the day floated by in a haze of early morning snuggles and a quick trip to the neighbouring town hospital for a bad case of diaper rash. I watched as my son sprawled across the carpet, busily playing with crumpled wrapping paper and a crayon covered card. This inaugural Father's Day seemed especially poignant. My heart beat with the familiar rhythm of joy and sorrow as I was reminded that this day was yet another milestone for our family, another checkmark in our year of tremendous firsts. More than just a celebration of my husband and the boys who made him a dad, this was also a day of mourning as we remembered the firstborn son who wasn't with us.

The lake water cast shimmering reflections through the window as I asked my husband about *his* experience with grief. He paused for a moment to think, and I was struck by the sudden realization that for the past year, his burden had been particularly heavy. As husband and father, his shoulders bore the weight of both his pain and mine. During an uncertain time, he stood tall as a protector, provider, and supporter, and he emerged from the other side stronger but still scarred. The sun streamed through the window and danced against the floral-patterned couch where we sat hand in hand, thinking back over the past year. I waited for my husband to speak, and when he did, he began by telling me of the moment he first held our stillborn son.

Seated alone in a hospital hallway, Andreas had watched as nurses hurried back and forth, their runners squeaking on the tile floor. Things had happened quickly, and he hadn't been allowed in the operating room. His nerves reverberated against his chest as he waited, anxiety building where hope and promise had once been. When the doctor emerged from the surgery silent and downcast, he immediately knew something was wrong.

They wrapped our firstborn in a pale green hospital towel and brought him to my husband—a tiny baby born breathless and still. Looking down at the silent infant in his arms, my husband felt powerless. This was an unsolvable problem, and there was nothing here for him to fix. Wishing to shelter his family from this searing pain, his protective nature screamed for a way to undo the loss and glue these fractured promises back together. Nothing could be done. He felt utterly helpless.

My husband is the family provider, and ready or not, he returned to work shortly after Landon's funeral. As protector and supporter, his list of duties was long: he spent his days at the office, his evenings at the hospital with our survivor, and his nights waking every three hours to help me clean breast pump parts. He cared for me during my postpartum recovery, came home early from work on my "bad days," and still managed to provide for us financially. Five months later, exhausted and emotionally drained, Andreas was worn down. He hadn't given himself enough time to fully process his grief and was reaching the end of his strength. Recognizing this, he took four weeks off work to regroup and spend time with family. This was a key part of our family's grieving process. We needed time to mourn together, communicate our pain, and lean on each other. Sadly, this is a luxury not all mourning parents get to share.

If you ask him, my husband is quick to point out the inconsistencies between a father and a mother's grief. In a society that struggles to appropriately deal with the pain of a loss, we sometimes forget to acknowledge that fathers need support too. There is more grace for the grieving mother's emotions than for the bereft father's. While differences in grieving styles between men and women may seem to indicate that fathers do not feel the loss of a child as acutely as the mother, this is not true. In a society where the words "be a man" are synonymous with shutting down one's emotions, fathers can feel a subconscious pressure to avoid tears or a genuine discussion of their feelings. But just because a father grieves differently than his wife doesn't mean he does not grieve.

As a mother, sharing my story has released a flood of similar experiences and commonly shared grief from the women around me. We find comfort as we discuss, rant, cry, and grow stronger together. From toddler play dates to online support groups, I have found an abundance of support and advice from genuine women with whom I share a common bond of loss. My husband has not found that. And on that sunny Father's Day, I finally thought to ask him about it: "Why? Why haven't you been able to find the same support that I have?"

Andreas simply shrugged and shook his head. "Maybe there aren't people who are grieving as I am."

It's easy to see why he feels alone in his grief. When sharing his story of loss with other men, the conversation is constantly redirected to lighter, more positive topics. Support for men simply doesn't exist in the same way; no one nods and tells him that they've "been there." It seems difficult for society to even acknowledge his loss.

Writing this, I'm once again reminded of how blessed I am to have a spouse who's willing to be open and transparent about his grief. This is what I've needed over the past couple of years: someone to talk with, lean on, and cry with. Side by side, we've ridden this rollercoaster of emotions together, both of us dealing with the loss in our own ways.

We were one of the fortunate couples who found that this loss drew us closer together, bonding and strengthening our marriage. But the heartbreaking truth is that for many couples, this is not the case. It can be extremely difficult to arrive at the place where we can grieve openly and honestly without hurting one another. The loss of a child places tremendous strain on marriages and relationships, and for some, it's just too much. As we work through our own grief, it's important to see how this loss affects those around us too. Our spouse is the one person that we should be able to turn to for constant support and understanding (and vice-versa), but differences in grieving styles often make this difficult to do.

While my husband's tears dried quicker than mine, it doesn't mean that his grief was any less. It simply means that his pain was most commonly expressed through different outlets. Because if there's one thing that I know for certain, it's that *infant loss affects fathers too*.

So that leads us to the question: How can we support our husbands? How can we continue to build up and strengthen our relationships in a time of such pain and hurt?

1. Don't Be Afraid to Ask for Help: Marriage/Grief Counselling

The world has been suddenly and irrevocably flipped upside down, and you find yourself in a fragile place of vulnerability and agony. Overwhelmed by a flood of new emotions and feelings, and battered and buffeted by waves of pain, you struggle to process everything. You feel angry, hurt, scared, lonely, depressed, numb … and like it or not, these emotions begin to carry over into the rest of your life, into the relationships with those closest to you. You're not sure how to put words to your pain. You argue with your husband. You feel misunderstood and alone. You see that your spouse is grieving too, but you find yourselves increasingly distant, and you don't know how to close that gap.

If this sounds familiar, you're not alone. A 2010 study confirmed that after a miscarriage or stillbirth, the risk of divorce or separation increases by over 20 per cent.[16] While there are countless other factors that play into

---

16 Katherine J. Gold, Ananda Sen, and Rodney A. Hayward, "Marriage and Cohabitation Outcomes After Pregnancy Loss," National Center for Biotechnology Information, accessed August 13, 2019, https://www.ncbi.nlm.nih.gov/pmc/articles/PMC2883880/.

the dissolution of a marriage, pregnancy loss can be a very clear stressor upon a relationship. When you're spending each day simply fighting for air to breathe, you may not feel as if there's strength enough left to fight for your marriage. The sharp bits and pieces of grief slowly wear away at the fabric of your relationship, and as these wounds multiply over time, it becomes harder and harder to repair what's been broken.

Attending counselling together (or individually) can be a really positive step for your marriage as you gain insight into your grief. Counsellors will be able to provide you with effective tools for communicating together, as well as work with you on individual issues that have arisen. There is no shame in asking for help. There's nothing wrong in admitting that you can't do it on your own. You hear stories of other couples drawn closer together because of their loss, and you may wonder, "Why doesn't it look like that for us?" But the reality is that none of our marriages are perfect. I know you've lost a lot already. I know that some days it feels easier to give up. But talk with someone about it first—you don't have to do this on your own.

2. Seek Honest and Intentional Communication

After an emergency C-section at twenty-eight weeks, Mandy's identical twin boys were brought into the world: one with heart failure, the other with kidney failure. Their son, Jasper, passed away the day after birth, and his brother, Michael Jr, followed three weeks later.

"My husband was very supportive throughout this whole process," Mandy shares. "We were able to talk about everything openly. He did have a lot of regret after deciding against putting our second son on life support. I didn't want to, but my husband did. It was made very clear to us by the neonatologist that our baby's condition was fatal, and I didn't want to prolong my son's suffering. My husband reluctantly went along with my decision. I felt that he kept a lot of his feelings inside so as not to upset me further, but I do feel that we have a stronger bond because of the trauma we experienced."

When it came to processing and working through her grief, Mandy says that her husband held a key role: "My husband let me talk and cry as much as I needed to. He was always open to talking about things and just really listened."

It can be difficult to sit and talk about the depths of your loss, but it's important to know where your spouse is when it comes to grief. It's important to recognize that both partners are grieving and that both need support. Communication isn't always verbal, and not all of us feel the need (or have the ability) to openly share our emotions. Many of us struggle to find words that adequately express the damage and uncertainty boiling inside. Try to set some time aside from the busyness of everyday life and just talk with your spouse. Be honest and intentional about your conversation: let your spouse know that you're grieving and you're hurt but that you still need each other. Don't be afraid to tell him how you're really feeling and to specify any ways you'd like support. In return, remember to ask him what he needs from you and stay open to his response. Ask each other questions like: How do you grieve? How can I support you in that? Is there anyone you can talk to about this fully? Do you want to talk to someone about this?

As a couple, find ways to help each other feel valued and heard—you are your spouse's main support, so love on them with all you've got.

3. Recognize That Your Husband May Grieve Differently Than You

After my first miscarriage, I felt a grief disconnect from my husband. I felt bloodied and empty, yet my husband seemed barely affected. Although he frequently talked about our stillbirth, this first-trimester loss seemed forgotten, her name hardly uttered. But just because I didn't see him grieve doesn't mean that he wasn't feeling the loss.

Amy shares a similar story after her five-week miscarriage: "I was told that I probably had a chemical pregnancy and that it happens a lot. I was devastated. My heart hurt badly, but I think what hurt the most was the fact that my husband (who isn't one to show a lot of emotion) seemed really nonchalant about it. He didn't say much at all. Since then, my husband has shared how he was heartbroken too but didn't know how to deal with it, with me, and with all of our emotions."

As mothers, we carry these little ones in our womb *and* in our hearts. From the very start, we feel our body changing and growing to protect and nurture this little being, and we bond with the baby much quicker than does our spouse. After a loss, women may carry literal scars and reminders of their pain. We may blame ourselves more acutely, feeling as if *our* body has failed us. Our pain may look different than that of our husband's, but although we stumble over different rocks, we're still hiking this mountain together. Your husband probably won't burst into tears at the sight of a pregnant woman or a baby onesie, and that's okay (just like it's okay if he does). There will be times when you may need to give each other space to grieve, but more frequently you'll need to lean on and support one another. Your spouse has strengths that you do not. As a couple, take this opportunity to recognize your differences and purposefully use them as a stepping stone for moving forward: *"Then the Lord God said, 'It is not good that the man should be alone; I will make him a helper fit for him'"* (Genesis 2:18).

4. Turn to Christ

And finally, if you take nothing else from this chapter, please hear this! Our marriages are nothing without Christ. Just as it's important for us to turn to Christ in our individual faith walk, it's equally important for us to lean into Christ as a couple. Let Christ be your centre. Walk alongside each other in your pain, spend time in the scriptures, and remain accountable to one another.

After the loss of our son Landon, my husband and I went through several months where we felt incredibly close to God. In our sorrow, we had nowhere else to turn. Our strength was sapped, our emotions frayed, and we found ourselves on our knees, crying out to Him for our every moment. A few months later, we both found ourselves in a place of lethargy. It wasn't as if we didn't know that God existed or that we weren't continuing to trust Him, we were both just tired. Our devotional time hit a slump, and we felt a lack of motivation to change things. Our grief had permeated our spiritual lives, but rather than using this time as an opportunity for renewal, we let it wear away at us.

During these difficult seasons, it's especially important to encourage and support one another in faith. Marriage is so much more than having someone to share your half of the rent or to raise children with—you were created to be in complete partnership both physically *and* spiritually.

Leaning on each other in times of weakness, we should actively and continually seek to remind our spouse of the cross. If one of us is struggling with faith, let us explore our questions together. Dive into God's Word and spend quality time together in prayer as a couple.

There is no doubt that grief sucks, but in this place of despondency there are still incredible opportunities for growth. Yes, grief has taught you about death, but it can also teach you so much about *life* and about what it means to truly live. Experiencing the death of a child means that you have gained an increased understanding of the depths and heights of love. Let this greater capacity for love transform your marriage and your relationship with Christ. Steeped in grace, come to the cross together.

> *But he said to me, "My grace is sufficient for you, for my power is made perfect in weakness." Therefore I will boast all the more gladly of my weaknesses, so that the power of Christ may rest upon me. For the sake of Christ, then, I am content with weaknesses, insults, hardships, persecutions, and calamities. For when I am weak, then I am strong.*
> —2 Corinthians 12:9–10

Some of you may come to the conclusion of this chapter and think, "Well, that's great for someone else, but ..." You have a whole list of reasons as to why this chapter doesn't feel particularly applicable. Perhaps you've already separated from your child's father. Perhaps you feel as if you've given, and given, and given, but never received anything in return—you're at the end of your patience. Or maybe you're wondering, "How can God redeem my marriage in the midst of this loss when my husband isn't even saved?" These are heavy questions to battle with, ones that don't have any clear-cut, definite answers. We wonder where we can find the strength to continue supporting someone who has hurt us, or what we should do when this support feels one-sided. How can we continue to love and care for our grieving spouse, no matter what our relationship currently looks like? What if the relationship was abusive or has since dissolved—does that impact or change the dynamic of our grief?

Rose was twenty years old when she found out she was pregnant. She had fallen in love with a nineteen-year-old boy who was using her solely to fulfill his own desires. "He didn't love me," Rose says with heartbreaking honesty. "We weren't dating, but he wanted sex. I was so desperate for love that I gave it to him without complaint. That was how I got pregnant." Rose moved back into her parents' home in order to get help with the baby, but at an eighteen-week appointment, the doctors discovered devastating news. Rose's baby had stopped growing two weeks earlier and there was no heartbeat.

"I was completely heartbroken," Rose says, "and I longed for something or someone to fill that hole." Rose spent three days in the hospital, giving birth to a lifeless child whom she would only get to hold for a few moments. "The father of my baby wanted nothing to do with me. Once I gave birth to the baby's body, he pushed me away. He actually admitted that he had a girlfriend while I was pregnant and that she was more excited for my baby than *he* was. I wasn't supported at all by him, and when the baby was gone, he seemed relieved. That destroyed me even more. I was on my own and completely broken. The only guy I had ever truly loved had just pushed me away and metaphorically spat on my face."

Today, Rose is married to an amazing, loving husband and has given birth to another beautiful son, but it has taken a long time for her to get to where she is. "It used to hurt so much that I wished I could change what had happened. During the time of the miscarriage, I had been struggling with mental illness for over seven years. I turned to psychiatric units and men to cure my pain. It didn't work. It took me another three years to begin to accept the fact that without this heartbreaking loss, I wouldn't have the life I have now. I wouldn't be married to my husband or have my second son. My life would have been completely different—and realistically, quite awful, given the situation. I still hurt for the loss of my baby, but I have accepted this hurt as a part of my life. I know that my son will never be forgotten by me or my family."

I really appreciate the truths found in Rose's story: baby loss doesn't just occur in happy, healthy marriages. Life can be incredibly messy, complicated, and confusing—and even more so when a miscarriage or stillbirth adds in additional heartbreak and emotion. I don't know where you are today in your relationship with your baby's father. You may feel loved and closer than ever, or your relationship may feel strained and drawn, or simply non-existent. No story is the same. No history is identical. As you reflect on this section, begin journaling through *your* experience. Our story doesn't always look the way we wanted it to, and we're not all going to fit a "how-to" guide for marriage after pregnancy loss. As you write, think about tangible ways you can move forward in a healthy manner. Spend some time writing out a prayer to God, asking Him to redeem, heal, and strengthen this relationship.

> *Above all, keep loving one another earnestly, since love covers a multitude of sins.*
> —1 Peter 4:8

Journaling Prompts
How Can We Support Our Grieving Partners?

- How has your spouse's/partner's grief differed from yours? How has it been similar?

- In what ways has this loss strengthened your relationship? In what ways has it hurt it? What areas of your relationship do you want to work on? Where do you see God's redeeming work within this relationship?

- Write a letter to your spouse/partner expressing your gratitude for the ways he's supported you. Tell him much you care, and let him know what you still need from him. Be open and honest about what you're feeling. Write down any emotions that you've experienced but haven't been able to talk about in person. Let this be as a love letter to him, the beatings of your heart echoing across the page. Consider asking him to write a similar letter in return.

Chapter Eight
Supporting Grieving Children

"We get to go to Heaven right now?" My almost-three-year-old looked up at me, eyes wide with equal parts confusion and anticipation. I could see the little wheels turning in his head as he added an excited follow-up question: "We get to go to Jesus's house?"

My heart broke. I just had finished explaining to him our plan for the day. A family friend had delivered a precious baby girl, and we were heading to their downtown apartment for a quick visit. We had watched this friend's belly stretch and grow over the past nine months, and I felt a particular bond with their newborn daughter. My friend and I had found out we were pregnant within days of each other, our due dates just a week apart—the only difference being that my pregnancy ended in the first trimester while hers went on to result in a beautiful, live birth at forty-one weeks. My son had watched her blossoming belly growing rounder and rounder over the past few months but was understandably confused by the part that came next.

"But why didn't the baby go to Heaven?" he asked as I loaded him into the car. I tried my best to correct his misunderstanding, but his confusion was valid. In his near three years of experience, my toddler has learned that babies don't come home from the hospital: babies are in a mommy's tummy one day and with Jesus the next.

I wish that my son never had to visit a grave marked with his brother's name. Grief is messy and complicated and comes with oh-so-many questions that I wish my son didn't know to ask. I wish he didn't know that some babies live in heaven and that sometimes we say good-bye before we say hello. But these sorts of heartbreaking conversations and questions aren't something that can be hidden away. Whether our children's grief is clearly demonstrated or not, pregnancy loss is a topic that affects the *entire* family.

Stefanie's Story

Two years after becoming parents, Stefanie and her husband were ready to try expanding their family once more. This time, the added excitement would be seeing their two-year-old enter the role of big sister. Stefanie says, "We conceived immediately and were incredibly excited. At the nine-week dating ultrasound, the technician was very quiet, only asking questions like, 'Have you had any cramping or bleeding?' I hadn't and began to feel uneasy. The technician couldn't tell me what she saw, and I left the appointment with the instructions to make a doctor's appointment for later that afternoon." Stefanie was in the early stages of a miscarriage. The doctor confirmed her greatest fear—there was no heartbeat.

Stefanie spent the morning sobbing into the carpet of her bedroom floor, the doctor's words echoing around her head and wounding her soul. "My husband and I grieved hard, and we grieved very differently," Stefanie says. "We secluded ourselves from others, and sometimes from each other. Seven months later we experienced our second miscarriage. Re-living the nightmare made it no easier. How could we be here again?"

Stefanie says that one conversation stuck out to her in particular: "How many times are we going to do this?" Stefanie's husband asked after their second loss.

"As many times as it takes to have two babies in our arms," she replied.

"I don't know if I can do that."

"Why?" Stefanie asked.

"Because each time I lose a piece of you," her husband responded.

With the help of an expanded medical team, Stefanie's fourth pregnancy was carried to term: two children in their arms, and two forever in their hearts. But Stefanie knows that the grief felt after a miscarriage doesn't just stop with the parents. It trickles down, touching upon each and every member of the family. Stefanie frequently writes and shares about the ways her daughter has grieved the loss of her siblings.

"My five-year-old had a lot of questions when we told her about the losses: 'Where are they? Where is Heaven? I want to go there. How can I go there? Will they come to my birthday? What are they doing in Heaven?'"

Stefanie says that when it comes to talking about the miscarriages, she usually follows her daughter's lead. "She knows they died in my womb. I don't offer all the details, and I try to keep it age appropriate for her. I share enough so that she has the general facts but not enough so that it would overwhelm her. She also knows that Mommy has other mommy friends with babies in Heaven. It's a fluid conversation that sometimes catches me off guard, but it's always welcomed."

Stefanie also wrote her daughter a social story about pregnancy loss, using real family photos. "She knows that when she's missing the babies, she can pull this book off the shelf and we can read the story about our family together."

Stefanie's eldest daughter talks about the "babies in Heaven" often. For them, conversations about her daughter's heavenly siblings will always be welcomed, even if it stings her heart to acknowledge this separation of their family. "I talk a lot more about Heaven than I used to, because half my children are there. My daughters' siblings are in heaven. This type of loss makes Heaven seem so much closer than it used to be. I know that one day we will all be together again."

You don't have to spend much time with Stefanie to see just how passionate she is about creating space for her children to grieve. It's an aspect of "life after loss" that we sometimes gloss over: the fact that this shared grief may change some of the everyday discussions or attitudes around the house.

For me, the realization that children understand and grieve more than we think they do occurred a few months after my son turned two. In preparation for a women's church retreat, I had been asked to film a short five-minute testimony about what my faith meant to me. Dragging along my son (and enough Goldfish crackers, crayons, and toys to keep a small army happy), I headed to the church mid-week to film. Settling him a few feet away from my chair but still out of camera range, I asked my son to play quietly for a few minutes while I talked.

The pastor in charge of the interviews set up the camera, and I began sharing the story of my twin boys and the resulting impact that the loss had had upon my faith. Everything seemed to be flowing smoothly until I noticed the pastor gesturing emphatically towards my son. My two-year-old hadn't made a sound, but seated quietly on the floor, a pile of untouched toys strewn around him, his face was lined with huge, rolling tears.

This wasn't the first time that he had broken down into tears upon hearing my testimony. A few weeks earlier, while sharing at an event for grieving families, my toddler began to silently sob. (Trust me, this is not how he normally cries!) My husband passed him over to me, and with him snuggled on my lap for the rest of the talk, I deviated from my script in order to share how infant loss affects our children too. Until that moment, however, I myself hadn't realized just how great his comprehension level really was.

Other parents have also noted that their children's initial responses to grief occurred much earlier than they'd thought it would.

Andrea says, "My son is only two years old, but I strongly believe that he has felt, to some degree, his own grief over the loss of his sibling. I believe he has also sensed my own grief. He has exhibited extreme separation anxiety and intense anger from a young age (despite us giving him a peaceful, nurturing environment). He has always been drastically more aggressive than other children his age."

Whether we realize it or not, children are very much in tune with their parents' emotions. Oftentimes a child's grief presents itself through varying behavioural symptoms, non-verbal reactions, and emotions such as anger, anxiety, tantrums, clinginess, fear, etc. Even if a child is too young to understand loss, they're still likely to pick up on the fact that their mother is upset. After my first miscarriage, for example, my son was very aware of my changing emotions. Even at two years old, he knew enough to question, "Where baby go?" or "Why mommy sick?" From the start, we had allowed him to be actively involved in my pregnancies (guessing the gender and attending doctor's visits), and it was therefore very important for us to include him in their loss.

How our children express their grief will vary from child to child, depending on their age, personality, developmental stage, family circumstances, how those around them are grieving, and how aware and interactive they were with the pregnancy. Naturally, our older children will be able to handle and process different depths of conversation than their younger siblings.

After the loss of one of her twin daughters, Kimberlee shares how her two children have had very different reactions to the loss of their sibling: "Piper's surviving twin is only three years old. She knows that her sister is with Jesus and doesn't really ask any further questions. My eight-year-old son, on the other hand, has a kind, sensitive heart and weeps when he looks at Piper's memory book and box. He thinks about how fun it would have been to have two little sisters to chase. He really cries about not being able to see Piper alive. We talk about the hope we have in Christ and that we will see her again someday; this has really encouraged him and has given him peace."

When helping your child process their grief, it's important to meet them where they're at emotionally and answer their questions directly and honestly. By creating this space for discussion and questions about grief, we let our children know that grief is healthy. We give our children permission to mourn by modelling grief for them. This is important, as it lets them know that it's good to *express* pain rather than suppress it. It's okay to tell them that "Mommy is feeling sad today because the baby went to be with Jesus. I miss the baby, and that's why Mommy's crying."

When Kristy and her husband lost their son, Luther, at thirty-nine weeks, the couple returned home from the hospital and had to explain to their very perceptive four-year-old son that the baby had died. "Our son listened solemnly and quietly, and when we were done, we told him it was okay to be sad. He collapsed into our arms and wept for several minutes. In the months that have followed, he has had many questions about the logistics of his brother in Heaven, and his ease of understanding and conversation in this tricky subject is so refreshing. I overheard him the other day having a conversation with his little friend about the new baby that is expected to be born to their family soon: 'That's nice that your mommy's having a baby. We had one too, but he died at the hospital. I sure hope your baby doesn't die!' When explaining the burial, we told him that his brother lived in Heaven but that he left his skin and skeleton behind like a little doll, and that we would plant it in the ground like a seed." Kristy adds with a smile, "He's a little boy who loves science and body questions, so this really isn't as vulgar or scary as it sounds!"

The kinds of questions your child asks will vary. For my two-year-old, it was enough for my son to simply know that his siblings were in Heaven. His questions about death went no further than, "Where did baby go?"

From the start, we were very open with him about our pregnancies. For months after my miscarriages, he would pause before sitting on my stomach and ask, "Baby in there, Mommy?" Only after I reminded him that the baby had gone to be with Jesus would he flop against me. While he's currently content with these simple questions and answers, I know there will be days in his future when he's forced to confront this loss. As he grows older, he'll have to find words for his own story. Drawing out his family tree for school, he'll have to decide whether or not to include his twin brother. Kids hanging upside down from monkey bars and adults standing in line at the grocery store will all ask him if he's "the oldest," or question, "How many siblings do you have?" He will have to choose how to reply. These are standard, everyday, get-to-know-you questions. Unfortunately, there just aren't any standard answers in our family.

Not all parents decide to talk openly about their loss. Some may decide to postpone that discussion until the child is older. "I miscarried during my first pregnancy," Tara-Lynn shares, "and my son is currently too young to understand. If he brings it up when he's older, I won't hide it, but I'm not sure if I'd bring up my loss before he's married."

As parents, it's important to discuss and research whether or not you plan on entering into this emotional space with your child. Although your child may still be too young to fully comprehend what has happened, with time you'll be able to broach the topic with more in-depth conversation.

Cassie says, "I'm not sure how I'll explain this loss to my son, but it's something that I'm sure I'll figure out as he grows older. I'm looking forward to that day, though. I'm excited to show him all the love we received from our family and friends, and to explain to him just how loved his sister was."

Losing someone you love is difficult no matter your age. As parents, our job is to be there for our children throughout the ups and downs and to model for them a healthy way to work through their grief. When my husband and I lost our firstborn twin, we made a conscious decision as a couple to be open about that loss from the very beginning. There was never a moment where we sat down and told our son about his twin brother; he has simply grown up always knowing about him. By the time he's able to fully understand this loss, he may feel that he has already sufficiently grieved, or he may require more time to process it. Regardless of the way he eventually acknowledges this grief, we as parents want to be there to support him, to be open, and to talk about it.

In our search for healing and strength, we've allowed ourselves the opportunity to grieve as a family. We celebrate and remember the lives of the littles we've lost, but our family doesn't revolve around this death—our focus is and always will be primarily on loving and parenting the giggling munchkins in our arms.

It's important to remember too that while we're helping our children process *their* grief, we need to be considerate of our *own* grief. Children don't always know when it's appropriate to bring up a difficult subject and may need to be re-directed until you're emotionally ready to answer.

My friend Rhonda reminded me of this when she said, "Our kids were very little when we miscarried: they were only one-and-a-half and three years old. They talk about it very matter-of-factly and ask what it was like. They want to know what they were doing at the time and how they responded. Now they're able to understand that this can lead to much sorrow and suffering. We talk about how it's important to be respectful but not to let someone else's sorrow or tears stop them from asking about a person's story."

As difficult as it is to walk this journey of grief with our children, we need to remember that we're not doing it on our own. The same gracious offer of "comfort for those who mourn" exists for our children too. These little ones hold a very special place in God's heart. In Mark 10:13–16, Jesus speaks clearly about not hindering our children from approaching Him, saying that, *"the Kingdom of God belongs to such as these"* (v. 14, NIV). The promises and security of God are just as vital and reachable for our children as they are for us as parents. Just as we model the basics of grief for our children, model Christ for them *in* that grief—give them the foundational tools they will need for the inevitable dark days that still lie ahead of them. As parents of grieving children, part of our role must include pointing our little ones to the One who makes us whole.

When teaching our children about grief and loss, keep it in eternal perspective. We grieve, but we do not remain *bound* to that sorrow. When we grieve, we grieve with hope.

Journaling Prompts

How Can We Support Our Grieving Children?

- In what ways have you seen your children grieve? How have/will you respond to difficult questions? These questions could include: Where is the baby? Why did the baby die? What happened to the baby's body? Will another baby die too?

- What worries or inadequacies do you feel when it comes to helping your children process their grief? How do you think this grief will touch upon their future (if at all)?

- What parenting style do you lean towards: do you discuss your loss with them or have you decided not to? What has brought you to that decision?

Chapter Nine
When Words Hurt

"At least he died as a baby. It's more painful to lose them when they're older."

My son's burial had concluded only moments earlier. The funeral home had set up a green, fabric canopy to protect us from the raindrops that dripped lazily from an overcast sky, and we huddled silently underneath as workers in construction vests tidied the area around the new grave. My grief was as fresh as the mound of dirt that covered my son's coffin.

"At least he died as a baby …" This was not something that I had wanted to hear. Not on this day, not ever. The sentence stung against my skin and irritated wounds that were still fresh. There was no comfort to be found in these words, but what made them all the more painful was that this unthoughtfully expressed comment was uttered by my beloved grandfather.

Forty years earlier, my grandad lost his son to a battle with leukemia. Growing up, I'd heard a lot about this Uncle Gordy: a funny, rambunctious, seven-year-old who'd led my grandparents to church before heading home to be with his beloved saviour. Each summer during the few weeks I spent at my grandparents' cabin by the lake, my grandad would share stories about the little blond-haired boy who stole a piece of his heart. Floating on buoys in the cool water, with hot sun sizzling against my skin, I'd listen as my grandfather shared stories about my uncle and my dad—the mischief and fights they'd get into, the love they shared. I'd listen as he shared about days of laughter and sorrow: the day Gordy was born, the day he was diagnosed, the day he died. Out there on the lake, my grandad often talked about the son whose memory they fought so hard to keep alive. Gordy was never far from their minds, and they longed for the day they'd be reunited with their son.

Because of this past, I'd expected my grandfather to be able to better empathize with the pain of losing my own son. But it was clear that Landon's gravesite service had brought back Grandad's own bitter memories of hospital visits and small-sized coffins. He was thinking about the death of a seven-year-old boy and the hurt that he'd carried for forty years. I knew that he didn't mean to be unfeeling in the midst of my grief; he was simply too caught up in his own world of pain, his own loss. His comment wasn't about *me* or *my son* at all—it was simply the truth as he knew it. But this didn't make his words sting any less, and it certainly didn't make them any more appropriate for that moment. I couldn't bear to tell my grandad that while it may have been "more painful" to lose an older child, I would still have given anything for a little extra time with my baby. I would have gone to the moon and back just to see my son take his first breath.

While I wish I could say that these types of comments are rare, it quickly became apparent that this wasn't the only insensitive comment I'd have to deal with. Loss parents are often faced with navigating a vast number of minefields during everyday conversations. Seemingly innocent questions such as, "How many kids do you have?" or "Are you planning on having more?" can trigger an avalanche of complex emotions. And the simple truth is that we don't always *want* to respond to these questions.

When someone asks if my son is my oldest child, a quick yes or no answer is easier than a long, time-consuming response. A simple "Yes" doesn't include the awkward pauses or lingering emotional toll that comes with the truth. Saying "No" feels less like a lie, but it also means potentially opening myself up to shocked, sympathetic looks and polite apologies for my loss if they press further. These are the balances that run through my head before I open my mouth. I know that the grocery store clerk or the woman at the bus stop aren't asking to hear the full truth—they're just making small talk. It's just that for me, these sorts of questions end up being anything but small.

As a parent who has experienced loss, you've probably already had to deal with these sorts of questions. If you haven't yet, you will. Sometimes these questions act as triggers, bringing with them a flood of emotion and pain. Sometimes they're just frustrating, and you wish that the world could see the little one that you carry in your heart. You wish that these questions weren't so darn difficult to answer. How do we answer these types of questions without feeling like we're betraying the child we lost? How do we tell people that we only have one child when our heart carries two or three or four? What do we say when people ask us if we're "planning on having more" when we've spent the past year miscarrying baby after baby?

Christy's Story

Christy and her husband had been married for five years when they decided that it was time to start a family. Shocked, they discovered that they were pregnant after just one cycle. But Christy was worried. "Soon after we found out, I became convinced I was going to miscarry. I was filled with fear and worried daily. I didn't feel pregnant at all. At nine weeks, I began to bleed, and I knew what it meant. I immediately called my midwife, and she brought me in for an ultrasound. There was no baby on the screen."

The sac on the ultrasound measured just five weeks, and Christy was told she had a blighted ovum. While her baby had stopped developing weeks earlier, her body didn't recognize it for another month.

Christy went home to miscarry naturally. "I didn't know what to expect," she shares. "I was in shock. I didn't know that I'd have mini contractions, and I didn't realize that I'd have to pass the sac I'd seen on the screen just hours earlier. That day I learned I could trust my body in labour, even if I felt I couldn't trust it to sustain a pregnancy."

Six months after this loss, the young couple got pregnant again. "I woke up at 3:00 a.m. to take a pregnancy test and was ecstatic when it turned positive. Needless to say, my husband and I couldn't fall back asleep that morning. I had my first ultrasound at nine weeks, and we saw a gorgeous, tiny baby and heard the heartbeat. It was such a relief." After that initial appointment and crossing into the second trimester, fear that they would lose this baby dissipated. At twenty weeks, Christy and her husband learned that they were having a girl. Her organs were forming correctly and she was meeting all of the appropriate measurement milestones. Unlike Christy's previous miscarriage, there was no inkling of anything wrong.

Christy says, "Shortly after that ultrasound, we gave her a name: Chloe Grace. My husband had wanted to name his daughter Chloe since high school, and I too loved the name. It was perfect."

It was just a few days after their twenty-eight-week ultrasound when Christy stopped feeling Chloe's usual flutters and kicks. Fearing the worst, she headed to the hospital to hear the words that every parent dreads: "Here's her heart. I'm sorry to tell you that it's not beating."

What word in the English language can even come close to describing the depth of that loss? After twenty-nine painful hours of induced labour, Chloe was born still. The tiny baby girl was buried in a beautiful gown that they had received from Little Angel Gowns. Christy shares the importance of this when she adds, "A year earlier, I had donated my wedding dress to them in honour my miscarried baby. It only seemed fitting."

While they had originally kept their miscarriage to themselves, only sharing the news with family and close friends, they didn't have that luxury after their stillbirth. Christy says, "We couldn't hide a loss that late, and I hated it. My grief was so raw and new, and I needed time to grieve before sharing it openly. What made it worse were people's ignorant comments. Now I talk about both my losses openly, but it really depends on the situation and the people. If I know someone won't handle it well, I don't share—not for their sake, but for mine. I'm still so sensitive to mean and uninformed comments."

After her stillbirth, Christy says that she found the interactions with people around her drastically changed. "People were awkward, insensitive, and thoughtless. It was hard to connect with them. People don't understand why I'm still grieving a year later, and they judge the way we choose to grieve. There was also a lot of silence and pretending like my loss didn't happen. They didn't know what to say, and I could no longer engage in their "petty" concerns or worries. What truly mattered in life became so apparent to us, but this wasn't the case for the people around us. They were still complaining about the little things, and I found that so difficult to be around."

A few weeks after my first miscarriage, I met a man in the grocery store who was quite impressed by how well my two-year-old son was behaving (not an everyday occurrence—trust me). The man smiled at my son and asked how old he was. Upon replying that my toddler had just turned two a couple of months before, the man proceeded to look pointedly at my flat belly and shake his head. "It's not good to have children so far apart. You should get pregnant again soon, because if the kids are more than three years apart, they'll fight."

I felt my face slide into a polite, frozen smile and nodded good-bye without another word. Despite the sting, it was not worth responding. This stranger had no way of knowing that just weeks earlier I'd been lying in a hospital room, watching all traces of my pregnancy and my baby's life slowly ebb away.

These kinds of questions and comments are not *intended* to cause pain. They're usually careless remarks spoken by someone who didn't take the time to think their thoughts through. Most of these questions are born out of curiosity, a desire to get to know someone better, or a need to fill empty air. And while the insensitivity of the man at the grocery store made me angry, the comments that bruise the deepest don't usually come from strangers—the statements that hurt the most tend to come from those who know and care about your loss.

Julie says, "I think the hardest comments for me to take are from well-meaning people who try to offer 'helpful' advice when I'm in an emotionally raw state. As someone who has struggled with unexplained infertility, I get it that we have to put up with strangers questioning our food choices, exercise habits, and asking us questions to make sure that we're not sniffing paint or carrying boxes over ten pounds. It's usually easy to see how those comments are coming from well-meaning people who truly care and don't mean to be hurtful. They simply don't realize that they just implied you caused your miscarriage by carrying an overstuffed briefcase to work every day."

If you've joined a grief group for loss parents, you've most likely heard some of the insensitive comments that grieving individuals have had lobbed at them by friends and acquaintances. These comments are usually variations of the same underlying themes: "Cheer up!" "Move on!" "Be thankful for what you have!" or "Don't worry—everything is going to be okay!" You may have been on the receiving end of some of these comments yourself. Rather than helping, these statements only seem to dig deep into an already tender wound.

Here are a few common remarks that grieving parents hear:

- "Man, can you imagine how tired you would have been with *another* baby?"
- "But you're young! Don't worry, you can try again!"
- "At least he died before you got to know him. It's harder to lose an older child."
- "You should just be thankful that you already have a kid!"
- "At least now you know you can get pregnant!"
- "Obviously God needed this baby more than you did!"

Hearing these kinds of careless remarks can be devastating. Friends and family often believe that these sentences are providing comfort or will ultimately help you find healing. They may not even realize that they've said something wrong. But while there are certain aspects of twisted truth buried amidst each of these tactless statements, this is obviously not the appropriate way or time to broach such topics.

"The worst for me," shares Joy, "was when a family member told me that it was a blessing in disguise that my Lydia had died. I carry a genetic disorder, and we found out after she had passed that she would have had it, and it would have been difficult to handle. I thought, *Are you serious? I wouldn't care if she was born with four arms! I love her because she was my baby.*"

After seven losses, Joy has had more than her share of insensitive comments. "I wish that someone would have told me about all the stupid comments I'd have to deal with. I feel like my choice to have more kids was taken away from me, and I wish that people would understand that not everyone gets a rainbow. It's hurtful when people try to argue or tell you that

'You'll get another baby! It could happen! Just have faith!' But if faith alone could have saved my babies, they would be here."

Upon reflection, Joy also shares the importance of protecting yourself in certain situations. She says, "As time has passed, I've been more hesitant to talk about these losses with strangers. Sometimes I feel like people aren't 'worthy' of knowing about my children. It's still my job as their momma to protect them."

We all know how easy it is to say the wrong thing when trying to comfort someone. Even individuals who work with grieving families every day can slip and make a thoughtless remark. While planning our son's burial, the funeral director floundered around for something comforting to say, and instead end up blurting out, "I can only imagine what you're going through. Just this past week our *cat* ran away! I don't know how I'm going to tell my son that Fluffy's not coming home." Hmm … somehow that story just didn't quite feel comparable to the pain surrounding the death of our son, and it *definitely* didn't seem like an appropriate anecdote to share while planning a baby's *funeral*.

Despite someone's best intentions, there will inevitably be moments when friends and family members speak before realizing the potential pain caused by their words. Before we lost our babies, it's likely that we too were once unaware of the pain that walked hand in hand with certain questions. Occasionally when meeting new moms, I find myself drifting back to these standard conversation starters. Countless times I've found myself tentatively asking, "How many kids do you have?" knowing only too well how difficult it may be to answer.

In contrast, there are many close friends and co-workers who fall on the other end of the spectrum: they simply don't say anything at all. You may find them ignoring your grief completely rather than talking about it. Afraid to say the wrong thing, they end up saying nothing at all, and you're left wondering why they're not being more supportive. Both ends of the extreme can leave you feeling vulnerable and wounded, alone in your grief and unsupported.

If you find yourself having to constantly answer a painful question, begin to prepare yourself in advance for how you will answer. Your answer may vary in different situations or on different days. Some days you may feel it's nobody's business, and other days you may want to shout the truth from the rooftops. Only you know how much information you feel comfortable sharing with strangers, acquaintances, or even friends. You don't owe anyone your child's memory, and you definitely don't have to feel guilty for wanting to keep them to yourself.

But regardless of the protections we place around ourselves, there will still be a day when the words pierce our armour and wound our already fragile-feeling skin. When this happens, try to keep in mind that your friends and family love you. They're not trying to *purposefully* create further pain; rather, their words are born out of a desire to help. Although these family members may not understand what you're going through or what you need to hear, the fact that they're talking about your grief at all shows their desire to support you.

"I try to tell myself that these comments are coming from a good place," Jessica says. "Do certain comments hurt? Yes. Does it sting when people don't talk about or recognize your loss? Yes. But these people have loved me my whole life. Why would I think now that they're intentionally trying to hurt me? I just have to keep reminding myself that they're responding the way they are because they're trying to protect me."

It takes strength to grieve honestly and to let people know what you do (or don't) need from them. When dealing with insensitive comments, it's okay to gently and lovingly correct someone.

For example, when someone says, "You can always try again for another one," take a deep breath and try your best to correct the insensitivity that lies at the root of that statement. This could look something like: "Yes, while my husband and I look forward to the day we can have more children, we also know that that's not always a certainty. Right now, we're mourning the loss of this precious child. This baby holds a place in our hearts that no future children will replace. Thank you for your support as we take time to grieve."

It's not always easy to respond with grace, and there will be days when you simply do not have the emotional strength to reply. There will always be callous and insensitive people in the world, but as we begin to advocate for ourselves, we build up communities of people who are better equipped to support the grieving families who come after us.

As a Canadian, I tend to kill people with kindness, but I also recognize that there are also occasions when you may need to be firmer with offensive individuals. Don't be afraid to speak up as often or as little as you need to. Don't be afraid to let friends and family know that you've been hurt by some of the comments they've made (and explain why). Sometimes you may need to ask someone who understands your grief (but is more removed from the loss) to help mediate this conversation. Our families won't always understand where we're coming from but hopefully, with careful reconsideration and honest conversations, they'll ultimately agree to stand alongside you.

As we educate those around us, we build a global network of individuals who are more intentionally conscious and thoughtful. Partnering alongside friends and family members who are sensitive to your loss will only serve to aid your grief process.

This is your grief journey. It's okay to stand up for it.

Journaling Prompts

How Do We Respond in the Midst of Pain?

- What are some of the most hurtful things people have said to you? Write them down and express the pain that they've caused. Look at each statement. Why was it so hurtful? How can you respond to statements like these in the future?

- Write a letter to those who have never experienced this type of grief. What do you want them to know about the words they say? How does it make you feel? What sort of things shouldn't they say? What sort of things should they say instead?

- Why do you think our society is so uncomfortable around grief? How can we help build a community of individuals who are more sensitive to the pain of those around them?

Chapter Ten

Holidays and Milestones

The faint sound of sleigh bells and Andy Williams' voice crooning, "It's the Most Wonderful Time of the Year" filled the small ultrasound room. I lay on my back and stared up at the speckled ceiling tiles, my heart fighting off the crumbly ache that comes with bad news. I wished that they'd just turn the music off.

It was ten days before Christmas, and we were miscarrying for the second time that year. It felt far from the "most wonderful time." While the world shone with twinkling lights and glittering snow, nothing around us felt very merry or bright. I stared at the ornaments hanging from the emergency room signs and watched as a paramedic in a Santa hat strolled down the hallway. I clutched at my stomach —the pain radiated from my empty uterus and echoed its way around my heart.

While it's difficult to say good-bye to a little one at any time of the year, the holiday season made me feel the sting of this loss all the more acutely. I should have had two twin boys racing around the house in reindeer jammies, excitedly tearing wrapping paper off boxed trucks and books. I should have been seven months into my second pregnancy, or I should have been three months pregnant with this one. These are the thoughts that circled continuously through my head as I watched another Christmas float by without three of my little ones. For every Christmas from now on, there would always be a handful of babies missing.

Holidays are just one of the many things that change after loss. Our perspectives alter and we often find ourselves reflecting on both what is and what could have been. For many parents, the first year after a loss proves the most challenging. Each month brings with it a wave of new developmental milestones, birthdays, anniversaries, and celebrations that would have been spent with our little ones. While subsequent years may prove difficult, there's something about having to face these holidays "alone" for the very first time.

Andrea, a mom who lost one of her twins in early pregnancy, says, "I always feel a twinge of pain on holidays and birthdays. I inevitably begin thinking that we should have been buying double the gifts, or I just end up imagining the two of my little ones playing together."

In addition to the holidays, many mothers struggle with facing special pregnancy milestones, such as the baby's due date, the day you found out you were pregnant, the day you discovered the gender, etc.

After my first miscarriage, I constantly thought about "how many weeks along" I would have been if things had been different. For months after the miscarriage, I'd open my email to find an annoying subscription from yet *another* pregnancy website (How many did I sign up for?) telling me that I was "entering my second trimester," when really my womb had been painfully empty for weeks. Seven months later, I found myself hovering around the calendar, anxiously watching for that first miscarriage's original due date.

As the day approached, I found myself increasingly emotional and reminiscent. The intensity of my grief surprised me, as I'd felt that I'd already had sufficient time to process my pain. I didn't realize how difficult this day was going to be. I couldn't stop thinking about what life would have been like if I hadn't miscarried Kära. I dreamed of expanding waistlines, tiny feet tangled in my ribcage, and days spent pacing around the house wishing my baby out. It seemed so long since I'd sobbed my good-bye, but out of all the pregnancy milestones, this was by far the most painful.

Tara-Lynn shares a similar experience after her first-trimester loss: "My baby's due date was October 19. I stayed home alone that day by choice and cried. I again felt like I was robbed of something that I had waited so long for and that it wasn't fair. I imagined what it would have been like if I was giving birth that day; I imagined a house filled with baby stuff and a big pregnant belly. I was heartbroken and sobbed all day."

When we lose a baby in our womb, we grieve for more than just our child—we mourn our future without them. We think about the "firsts" that we're missing, all the dreams and plans we'd hoped to share with our child.

Beyond the usual grief surrounding the loss of our baby, these anniversaries force us to confront the memories that we never got to create. As you carried this tiny babe in your womb, you began dreaming of snowy Christmas Eve's, chocolate Easter egg hunts, and adorable Halloween costumes. You dreamt of the Mother's Day cards you'd one day receive, the flowers they'd give you on your birthday, and the frosted cake you'd make for theirs. You pictured their high school graduation and imagined them walking across the gymnasium stage to collect their diploma. You thought about their first steps, their wedding day, or the day that they'd make you a grandparent.

Now, you have none of that. All you have to hold on to are dreams and memories that you never got to create. You desperately wanted to share these special moments with your little one, but now each holiday cruelly forces you to mourn these unborn wishes. And perhaps the worst of all these holidays is the one you had looked forward to so dearly: Mother's Day.

Mother's Day can be particularly difficult, as all of our crushed dreams and dashed hopes are laid out so clearly before us. Even if we have living children, the weight of those that are missing can still be felt so clearly.

"My first Mother's Day was horrible," Stefanie shares. "I deliberately skipped church, knowing that they would acknowledge the moms somehow. Even though I had one living child at that time, the pain was still too much. I knew that I was missing two babies from my arms, and that grief overwhelmed me."

Elizabeth also shares the story of her first Mother's Day: "It was my first Mother's Day after the loss of my daughter, June. My husband, mother, and I had a gentle day together and then went to visit my grandfather and his girlfriend. After greeting each other with hugs and wishing his girlfriend a happy Mother's Day, she turned to my mother and responded, 'Happy Mother's Day to you too!' My mother thanked her and then reminded her that even though my daughter, June, wasn't here, it was *my* first Mother's Day too. My grandfather's girlfriend turned to me, looked me up and down, and then turned away. She refuses to acknowledge that my daughter existed and that I am *indeed* a mother. Nothing has ever made my blood boil more than that."

Ten months after my son's stillbirth, I too realized that my first Mother's Day after loss was rapidly approaching. I went through the day in that strange blend of simultaneous celebration and grief, laughter and mourning.

And as the sun sank beyond the horizon, I sat down on my bed and wrote this journal entry: it was a celebration of the little lives that made me a mother and a cry from the depth of my heart as I mourned the memories that were never to be.

From my Journal, May 2015:

> Today is Mother's Day. Last year, I spent the day with four little feet squirming and pressing against my rounded belly. I imagined what this day would look like, what all future Mother's Days would look like. I dreamed of breakfast in bed, late morning giggles, and bear hugs as we sloshed orange juice on the duvet. I envisioned tickling twenty tiny toes and kissing the foreheads of two squirmy sons as we planned a family adventure involving ice cream and lots of laughter. There would be the inevitable scrapes and bumps, tears and frustrations, but those would be gently bandaged and rocked away in Mom's comforting arms.
>
> I knew there would be freshly picked flowers: a bouquet composed mostly of dandelions, daisies, and a lot of love. Two pairs of muddy boots would sit in the hall while fistfuls of blossoms would float lovingly in a glass vase. I never dreamed that one twin would have to pick them on his own. I never thought that I would be the one laying a bouquet on a grassy, infant-sized grave.
>
> This day is equal parts bitter, equal parts sweet. Today is my first Mother's Day with one baby, my first without the other.
>
> Gazing in from the outside, my arms do not appear empty. They are usually wrapped tightly around a beautiful and delightfully inquisitive baby boy. I am beyond thankful for this miracle. I hope that my arms will never be unoccupied and that the future will be filled with additional wee ones. But even if my lap is overflowing with curly-headed babes, even if my arms are never physically empty, they can never be completely full either.

> There will always be a part of me that longs to carry the additional weight of a much-loved infant. I miss that little one. I mourn for the baby that never fell asleep in the safety of his mother's arms, or heard his mother whisper just how much she loved him.
>
> For our family, someone will always be physically missing: a little voice that I will never get to hear, tiny hands that I will never get to hold. But no matter the earthly years that separate us, I will always be his mother. I can think of no sweeter thing than knowing that I carried and protected my son for the entirety of his life. While I do not carry out the everyday act of mothering two children, I will always be the mom of twins.

Experiencing these milestones for the first time can be devastatingly painful. The reality of our loss is once again forcefully flung in our face. Pregnancy milestones, due dates, loss dates, Mother's Day, seasonal holidays (and the list goes on and on) are naturally going to be more difficult than other days. Be patient with yourself and allow yourself time to grieve and mourn the memories that you never got to create. As hard as it is to cry yourself through Christmas Day, it's better to mourn than to ignore that pain completely. Your holidays may be filled with soggy eyes and damp tissues, but this doesn't mean that it was wasted time.

As you read through this chapter, take a look through the next few months on the calendar and mark down any days that may be "trigger days" for you (due dates, birthdays, holidays, Mother's Day, etc.). Give your spouse (or closest friends and family) advance notice that these might be rough days and that you may need a little bit of extra love and support. When you know that these dates are approaching, ask your loved ones if they would send a text message or a quick phone call to check up on you. Book a manicure or a massage, or ask a friend to take you out for coffee—whatever you need to do to pamper and take care of yourself. I know that it's uncomfortable to ask for help or to so clearly lay out what you need. You may feel that your friends and family should *know* what you need without asking, but oftentimes those around us are simply afraid to overstep their bounds, and they worry about unintentionally causing extra pain.

As in all areas of grief, give yourself grace. Having learned the importance of grace, and avoiding placing expectations on those around us, loss mother Jessica says, "Allow yourself permission to cry. Give yourself time. We all like to think that people know what we want or need, but they don't. Be careful about placing these expectations on others—it's dangerous. Sit down with friends and family and talk about what you would like these holidays to look like. Share things you desire to happen or things you want to avoid."

Jessica's right—you don't have to go through the holidays and milestones alone. Communicating and setting up care in advance will ensure that you have the support you need to carry you through the difficult days.

Another beautiful example of this was shared by Julie and her husband. On the anniversary of their loss, Julie's husband intentionally set aside some quiet time for him and his wife. Knowing just how difficult of a day it would be, he carefully planned a date to the campground where they had been when Julie had first started bleeding one year earlier. Julie says, "We made a campfire, watched the gorgeous sunset, and talked about the ups and downs of the past year and our miscarriages. It was actually really special."

This is an important thing to remember: despite the grief accompanying them, these milestones and holidays *can* be special. There's no doubt that these specific dates can be painful reminders of what we've lost, but in the fullness of Christ, they can also be beautiful reflections of God's continued grace in our lives.

It's easy to feel alone or forgotten on the holidays, to stumble into a pattern of envy for what we do not have, or self-pity for all that has been taken from us. But Christ has not abandoned us to our pain. The entirety of Jesus's ministry here on earth was spent walking amongst the sick and the grieving, the widows, the lepers, and the outcasts. He sat and shared bread with aching, sinful, and oh-so-broken men and women like you and like me. In the depths of their pain and separation from God, He *saw* them.

He came for them. He came for *us*.

Look for a moment at Luke 8:38–43, the story of the woman who had been bleeding for *twelve* years. Desperate and hurting, she comes before

Jesus, trembling and hoping. She knows that it would be enough to just touch His cloak and then quietly slip away amongst the crowds—but it's not enough for Jesus. Surrounded by a jostling mass of people, bumped and pressed by elbows and shoulders, Jesus feels her touch on the fringe of His cloak and He stops. He stops and calls out for her. He stops to look her in the eyes, to truly *see* her when no one else does. He stops to call her "daughter."

He does the same for you and me. He stops to look us in the eyes, to acknowledge the depths of our pain and our hurt, and to whisper to our aching hearts: "Daughter, your faith has made you well." These words don't negate the pain we have felt or erase the painful experiences that we've walked through, but rather they speak to the promise of something *more*, something *bigger*.

The King James Version says, "*Your faith has made you whole.*". Whole. What a beautiful word! What was once broken and unclean, stained by sin and death, has been not only repaired but *transformed*.

Psalm 56:8 says, "*You keep track of all my sorrows. You have collected all my tears in your bottle. You have recorded each one in your book*" (NLT). As we wait on the fulfillment of all God's promises, we walk through an earthly life filled with both joy and pain. Throughout these highs and lows, we can walk with the reassurance that we are not alone. There is no tear that escapes sight from the Lord. We have been *seen in our entirety*. And even more gloriously still, not only have we been seen, we have been *redeemed* by the power of Christ on the cross.

Julie's Story

By the time her second Mother's Day rolled around, Julie had experienced three miscarriages. Fighting to choose thankfulness on a holiday she would just rather avoid, Julie was given a beautiful reminder of just how closely God walks this road with us, of how He sees our pain, and how He knows the details of our loss intimately. Julie shares how on this Mother's Day morning, God gifted her with three precious bouquets of flowers, one for each of her three miscarriages.

"The Sunday school children at church planted impatiens flowers in cups to give to their mothers. I was helping with this project, and afterwards my friend gave me *two* boxes of impatiens to take home." This was especially significant, as Julie's first miscarriage occurred while she was pregnant with twins. Julie continues, "Then, while we were at a friend's house for lunch, I was surprised with an extravagant bouquet of flowers. My second miscarriage was by far the hardest, and it was as if God was saying, 'I know how hard it has been, and still is, for you to lose Keturah in your second miscarriage. I'm giving you a bigger bouquet to let you know that I understand that the depth of pain you carry from that is greater than the others.'"

Julie's third miscarriage happened early on in the pregnancy and was, therefore, a much quieter ordeal; the third flower she was given reflected that too. "Later in the afternoon, as my husband was standing out in our yard, a stranger drove past in a truck. He slowed to a stop, gave my husband a bottle with a single rose in it, and said, 'Here, you should give this to your wife.'"

The special significance of these three bouquets stuck out to Julie and her husband. After giving her the rose in the bottle, her husband mused, "You know, Julie, today on Mother's Day, God gave you three sets of flowers for each of the three miscarriages we went through. The first gift of flowers was even two boxes, for when we lost the twins."

Tears came to Julie's eyes, and she felt the wounds in her soul mend a little more. On the day that she felt she could not celebrate being a mother, God showed up and so tenderly acknowledged her personal pain and loss. He orchestrated the tiniest of details to speak the truth of His presence in and over her life. Julie says, "I share this story because I am amazed at the God we serve. A God who steps in to meet us in our pain and says, 'I love you, I care about *all* that you are going through, and I have not forgotten your pain.'"

> *Sing for joy, O heavens! Rejoice, O earth! Burst into song, O mountains! For the Lord has comforted his people and will have compassion on them in their suffering. Yet Jerusalem says, "The Lord has deserted us; the Lord has forgotten us." "Never! Can a mother forget her nursing child? Can she feel no love for the child she has borne? But even if that were possible, I would not forget you! See, I have written your name on the palms of my hands. Always in my mind is a picture of Jerusalem's walls in ruins.*
> —Isaiah 49:13–16, NLT

These verses in Isaiah speak to the promise of Israel's restoration, but they also show us a picture of just how tender God's compassion is for His people. Cling to this. As deep as your love for these little ones is, God's love is *always* deeper still.

He sees you. He sees your most difficult days. And He is *here*.

Journaling Prompts

When the Holidays Suck

- What holidays or milestones do you think will be (or have been) the hardest? What are some ways that you can begin building support for yourself now in preparation for those trigger days? Who can you ask to be by your side?

- In your grief, are you taking time to care for yourself? Why or why not? What will help you to feel loved and supported during this time?

- What memories did you hope to create with your little one that you're now missing out on? Some parents find it helpful to write letters to their little one. If you feel this will be beneficial for you, write a letter to your baby and tell them of all the things you'd hoped to share with them.

Chapter Eleven
Finding Ways to Remember

Sometimes it feels as if the whole world has forgotten your little one. You wonder if you're the only one who remembers their name, the only one who cares about that sweet feeling of life in your belly. The existence of this precious child pressed irrevocably against your heart and spun your life around. How could everyone else fail to remember such a poignant moment in time? On days like this, I'd find myself whispering my son's name aloud, the syllables disappearing into the empty room, just to hear someone say it. I needed to spend a few moments remembering the little life that touched my heart so briefly yet so profoundly.

Most of us don't worry about *completely* forgetting our little ones. We know that the babies who nestled within our womb will never be forgotten. Their memories will be buried deep within our heart, their names forever lying at the forefront of our tongue. They own a place in our family forever—it just looks a little different than we thought it would. But perhaps we're unwittingly influenced by this fear to a far lesser degree: we crave tangible reminders of the child we once carried because we don't have anything else. We know we won't forget, but what if these memories begin to fade? What if time smooths the sharp edges of our recollections, and the tiny face that was once so clear begins to blur? Perhaps already the pain we once felt has been polished away to a dull shine, and the tears that were once so quick to fall have begun to dry. At least when that grief was sharp and fresh, we knew that their memories were vivid and present.

We carry these scars on our hearts, but how can we show them to those around us? How can we ensure that we're not the only one who remembers them? How can we show the world around us *just* how much they mean to us and just how *long-lasting* their impact is?

And so we arrive at one of the great challenges after pregnancy loss: How can we find ways to adequately remember and celebrate the life of our child? How do we navigate holidays and birthdays, due dates or loss dates? Will we continue to celebrate these milestones a year from now? Five years? Twenty years? How do we walk through life in a way that ensures our child's memory will be kept alive? These are questions that loss parents wrestle with as they begin the journey of living each day without the one they love.

After my son's stillbirth, I felt incredibly moved by the multitude of small acts and soft-spoken words I received from friends and family. People around me went out of their way to include Landon and make special memories with him. My husband's cousins are particularly good at remembering. During our first Christmas after loss, they brought over gifts for our entire family, including a little burlap stocking for Landon. Other friends brought much-loved Willow Tree ornaments for my bookshelf or drove to the cemetery and laid flowers at his grave.

This experience was very different from my subsequent two miscarriages. With my first trimester losses, there was no cemetery to visit and no physical stone to mark their existence. These babies seemed to hover on the edge of acknowledgement. I received bouquets of flowers but no cards with their names on it or memorial trinkets for my shelf. With fewer tangible moments to cling to, it felt as if these losses were somehow less concrete than my son's stillbirth.

And yet there were a few key individuals throughout my loss journey who continually brought me to tears with their thoughtfulness and inclusion. My second miscarriage occurred a week and a half before Christmas. Relaxing at my parents' place, I was moved to tears when I spotted a new ornament hanging on their plastic, green-needled tree. A collection of snowy moose hung from a red string, a personalized name marking each animal: Grannie, Gramps, Landon, Alistair, Kära, and Björn. At that time, three of their four grandchildren were in heaven, but they had purposefully included all of them in the Christmas festivities. They don't hesitate to list them as grandbabies; they don't hesitate to remember them.

These are the things that hit deep: simple actions of love from those who first loved us and who, therefore, love our unborn babies too. In our grief, it's natural to want to find ways to remember the life of the one we've lost, to continue to honour and love them even in death.

In Mark 16:1–3, we read about the women who came to Jesus's tomb after His crucifixion, bearing spices that they had prepared[17] in order to anoint His body. The book of John[18] tells us that Jesus's body had already been bound in linen cloths and seventy-five pounds of spices. And yet the morning after the Sabbath, these women came anyway, hands weighted down with costly spices and oils. Mark says:

When the Sabbath was past, Mary Magdalene, Mary the mother of James, and Salome bought spices, so that they might go and anoint him. And very early on the first day of the week, when the sun had risen, they went to the tomb. And they were saying to one another, "Who will roll away the stone for us from the entrance of the tomb?"

On first glance, it seems silly for them to have come at all. They couldn't have possibly moved the stone on their own, Jesus has already been wrapped and buried in spice, and His body has been in the grave for three days. What did they hope to accomplish? What drove them to His tomb so early in the morning? If they had fully understood what Jesus had said about rising again, they wouldn't have come bearing spices at all—they would have known that it wasn't needed. They didn't come because they understood what was about to happen or the prophecies that were being fulfilled; no, they came solely because they loved. They came because their hearts needed to show the outpouring of their grief in tender, physical action.

By no means is this a perfect comparison for our own expressions of grief, but I think it speaks to the motivation behind those who mourn. God gave the great ability to love: an ability that can carry a tremendous amount of weight with it when the object of our affections is taken away. Earlier, in Mark 12:30–31, Jesus speaks of the greatest commandments:

---

17 Cf. Luke 24:1.

18 John 19:39–40.

"And you shall love the Lord your God with all your heart and with all your soul and with all your mind and with all your strength." The second is this: "You shall love your neighbour as yourself." There is no other commandment greater than these.

We are called to live a life of love. And while life may disappear overnight, the love that we hold for that individual will not—and God understands that. This is the essence of why we mourn—not because death is something to be feared, but because we've been separated from those we love. As we grieve and remember our unborn babies, we proclaim the value and the worth of the life that God has created. As we carry out these acts of remembrance, we are declaring the glory of God by celebrating and honouring the beauty, intricacy, and worth of His work. This is part of the great gift we have as children of God—the ability to glorify Him in *all* aspects of our lives, including our grief.

So with the understanding that these acts of grief are ways to both demonstrate love and glorify God, let me suggest to you three different ways that we can remember and honour the lives of our little ones:

1. Find Ways to Remember Alongside *Your* Family

When thinking of ways to remember your baby, spend some time in discussion with your spouse and children. Ask yourselves: How do we want to remember this little one? What is important to each of us individually? What is important to us as a whole family? There are many beautiful and creative ways to remember a pregnancy loss. Here are just a few examples of ways that families might choose to celebrate their little one's life:

- planting a tree or flower
- creating a small garden waterfall
- purchasing a plaque "in memory of"
- throwing a "birthday" party
- writing their name in the sand
- ordering a special teddy bear or personalized ornament
- a balloon release

- taking family photos with the shadow of your child edited in
- artwork created together as a family
- an annual trip to a favourite spot

Setting time aside to specifically reflect on your loved one will be helpful for both your and your family's grieving process. Remember that just as individuals mourn differently, so do families. What works for someone else may not work for you. Find an activity that is *meaningful for your family* and use that time to talk about the memories you have (or had hoped to make) with your baby.

Kimberlee and her family are a good example of this. I first met this fellow twin mom online after she wrote to me and shared a bit of her story. During that initial interaction, she also shared with me about the importance of remembering her daughter, Piper, not only for herself and for her husband, but as a way to support her surviving twin daughter. I thought that this was such an important and beautiful way of approaching remembrance—as an act that involves the entire family.

After the birth of a healthy baby boy, Kimberlee and her husband went on to experience three early miscarriages. Deciding to try just once more, they became pregnant with twin girls: Aubree and Piper. Early on in the pregnancy, it was discovered that Piper's amniotic sac was ruptured, which resulted in severely underdeveloped lungs. She was not expected to survive. Due to this rupture, Kimberlee went into labour at just twenty-seven weeks. Aubree was rushed to the NICU and did wonderfully, but Piper passed just an hour after birth.

Kimberlee says that first and foremost, her faith helped her to work through her grief. Also hugely important to her was the making of a baby book for Piper after she'd passed. "The hospital provided this special book, and it was a place where my husband and I could pour our hearts out for our daughter and celebrate her short life." This book is one of the ways that Kimberlee feels has helped her embrace her grief. "I open Piper's memory box and book and look at each thing, reading each word, and just let myself cry and cry until the tears run out and I know that she is not forgotten."

These tangible reminders, such as memory boxes, are often important parts of our grief journey. In our home, we've set aside a shelf in the bookcase where we keep a photograph of Landon and several Willow Tree ornaments symbolizing each loss. Not only do these mementos help me feel close to my missing children, they encourage conversation with those who visit us. I love being able to talk about *all* my children when the occasion arises, and having a few visible reminders of their existence gives houseguests the permission and freedom to speak openly about my loss.

At the same time, it's important for us to be mindful of the objects we keep in our home. Depending on how far along you were in your pregnancy, you may have already set up the nursery or bought a stroller and baby supplies. These items may be helpful grieving tools for you, but they could just as easily hinder or aggravate the process. Some items may need to be placed in storage for a time or returned to the store.

Keep in mind that your spouse (or other family members) may have a very different reaction to these items than you do. As your spouse grieves alongside you, continue to cultivate open discussion about what you need and why you feel it's important. Be willing to support each other as you make decisions about family remembrance activities or remembrance objects placed around the home. You may find that you and your spouse place significance on different things. That's okay (and completely normal.) As you encounter these differences, try to find common ground and ways to embrace your loss together.

Be as creative as you like when coming up with remembrance ideas. Some families prefer outdoor activities, like leaving a rock memorial on a hike, or walking along the beach and leaving the child's name written on a shell. Sarah's family, for example, released butterflies at the cemetery on their son's first birthday, and Joy's family releases lanterns on birthdays and makes cupcakes. Other families may rather spend time creating a baby scrapbook or knitting baby hats for a local hospital. Over time, these acts may evolve into an annual tradition, or you may choose to vary activities year to year.

Our family is definitely a family that thrives on traditions, and we have decided to set aside a specific day each year for remembrance. After my first pregnancy loss, I struggled with how to celebrate one twin's birthday while simultaneously mourning the other twin's loss date. I didn't feel that it was fair for my surviving twin, Alistair, to be continually reminded of his brother's death *on* his birthday. Because of this, our family decided to stretch the celebrations out over two separate days: Alistair would be celebrated on the boys' actual birthday, and we would remember Landon two weeks later, on August 12. This date was significant for us, as it was the day of Landon's funeral. Every year we set that date aside as a designated "family day." It doesn't matter what we do that day; all that matters is that we spend time together laughing, praying, mourning, and remembering.

Some families need these annual traditions, while others don't. Rhonda and her family planted blueberry bushes after her miscarriage—one plant for each person in their family, including the lost baby. On the due date, they bought helium balloons, one for each person, and wrote a note or drew a picture and tied it to the balloons. But for them, this was a one-time event, not an annual occasion. This is similar for Lindsey too, who says, "I haven't done anything significant in remembrance, except that on their due dates and loss dates, I stop and think about them."

The way we remember will be unique to each family. It doesn't matter how big the act of remembrance is, how frequently you participate in it, or whether you purposefully set aside time to remember or not. The point of these acts is that your family finds a way to share and demonstrate their love, all the while continuing to process rather than hide from grief.

2. Find Ways to Remember Alongside *Other* Grieving Families

Another important aspect in remembering our lost babies is to join together with other grieving families. Sometimes this involves participating in a fundraiser, a local grief share chapter, or a public event at your hospital. Particularly during the month of October,[19] many towns, states, provinces, or countries hold organized events for grieving parents. These public acts of remembrance can also be great invitations for friends or family members who want to support and grieve with you, but may not know how to get involved. Our grief is not a burden to be carried alone; gathering alongside other individuals strengthens and encourages these bonds.

---

19 October is Pregnancy & Infant Loss Awareness Month.

Many of the families I've spoken with participate in walks to raise awareness and partner alongside other grieving parents. Jessica says, "We have done a walk, and have a brick inscribed with our baby's name. We don't have a gravesite to go to, so I feel these sorts of events are good for my healing."

Meg and her husband also partner alongside new or grieving mothers, just in a slightly different way: "I do feel that my daughter may be forgotten, and that's why my husband and I still celebrate her. Each year on her birthday, we donate money to a cause that helps new mothers across the globe."

It's important to stand alongside each other—not only for our own sake but for others too. After my first miscarriage, I was extremely honoured to be asked to share a bit of our story at a church event for families touched by pregnancy or infant loss. Many churches are hesitant to touch upon this subject, and I was beyond excited to see the body of Christ opening up to taboo topics and embracing hurting individuals. The event was intimate and personal. We talked and we cried and we remembered. The table at the front was laden with sandwiches and homemade desserts to fill our bellies, and another at the side was loaded with pregnancy loss books and resources to give solace to our hearts. Some of us shared; some of us listened. Some of us were meeting for the first time, but all of us had a personal knowledge of grief and a bond that allowed us to authentically mourn and celebrate together.

Towards the end of this event, we carefully folded scraps of paper into rubbery, helium balloons and released them into the overcast sky above. They floated from our hands and carried our prayers, poems, and babies' names with them. There was so much beauty to be found in this simple act, and there is something to be said about the physical act of releasing a balloon (and all that it symbolizes for you) into the heavens. As I stood there, watching these little white dots disappear against the grey bank of clouds, I couldn't help but wish that there were more events like this—more opportunities for women and families to gather together, share their stories, and mourn as a community. This is a firsthand, practical opportunity to follow the command we read in Mark 12:31: *"You shall love your neighbour as yourself."*

If you have the chance to gather together with other loss families, I encourage you to do so. I know that some of us are introverts and others of us just hate opening up about emotions, but these are the individuals who will understand your pain on a deeper level. While we can take great comfort in the fact that there is a heavenly Father who understands us *perfectly*, we can also take comfort in the fact that He has called us to be in relationship with, and given us the ability to minister to, one another. Love on these dear hurting friends as best you can, lean on each other, and point each other to Christ. And in return, amidst this collective community of aching hearts, I know that you too will find great encouragement.

3. Find Ways to Remember on Your Own

Finally, let's talk for a moment about finding ways to remember on our own. As we grieve, it's crucial to find this soft balance between mourning alongside others and mourning by yourself. Some of you cringe at the thought of having to "remember on your own," while others can think of nothing better. For some of us, this is an everyday event. For others, being alone is equated with boredom and loneliness, depression or anxiety. But remembering on your own does not mean being lonely; remembering on your own means setting time aside to process and mourn in an authentic and direct manner.

At first glance, remembering on your own may seem like a strange concept. For me, it seemed that any time I had a spare moment to myself, I couldn't stop thinking about them! Why would I need to set aside *extra* time? But being purposeful about your grief is important. Reflection isn't something that can be rushed. Take a mini-getaway, or simply go for a walk by yourself. Write a poem or a song, hike, swim, run, paint, sketch, scrapbook or quilt—however God has gifted and talented you, use that as a way to release your grief. Purchasing jewellery or getting a tattoo are also common, physical reminders that many parents choose as a way to carry these memories with them daily.

Carla's Story

Carla was just one of the many women I interviewed who purchased jewellery as a way to remember and commemorate their loss. After the loss of her baby, Carla got a "baby bean" ring that she wears every day, and it's clear to see just how deeply she treasures it.

It was just a week after their positive pregnancy test when Carla first started spotting. Diagnosed with a "threatened miscarriage," Carla's worried heart was not at all encouraged by the doctor's sad statistics. They lost the baby two hours after their ultrasound.

"I had gotten back to work and when I stood up at my desk to go to the bathroom, I felt a somewhat familiar rush of blood. It was as if I was starting my period, but this time it was *a lot* of blood. I ran to the restroom to find my long underwear and dark wash jeans *drenched* in blood. I saw some tissue in the toilet and remember thinking, *Is that my baby? What should I do? Should I pull him/her out of the toilet?* And then, *Should I stay at work? How do I tell my boss I need to leave?*"

Fortunately, when Carla returned to her desk, her boss took one look at her and immediately told her to go home and rest. Her husband said he would be home soon but was preparing to go to China the next day and couldn't leave work right away. "The contractions came in full force when I got home," she shares. "I tried to ease the pain and the bleeding by jumping in the shower, but I learned that unlike period blood, miscarriage blood does not stop in the water."

The next morning, Carla's husband left for China and was gone for over two weeks. "I bled onto the carpet in the living room and I couldn't bear to clean it up," Carla says. "I spent that weekend away at my mom and cousin's. I bled for six weeks. I was a literal mess. That following May, I bought a ring to commemorate "Baby Bean." I still wear it every day, now together with the birthstone ring I have for our first son. I still miss Bean and wonder if he/she will know me whenever we meet again."

Around the time that she got her baby bean ring, Carla realized how blessed she is to have experienced the profundity of a lost baby. "I get to meet that baby in Heaven!" she says with oh-so-much excitement. "I am truly blessed. We will meet our children again, not in *this* life but the next. My understanding of eternity (that it exists and that we are destined for it) is what helps me cope with this grief. I mourn less because I know that I'll meet my baby again."

This feeling of being "blessed" in the midst of our grief isn't an easy place to get to, but in our grief we can still praise God for the cherished child He has bestowed on us. Setting aside moments for deliberate remembrance and celebration is one way of finding joy in the pain. By choosing to remember the precious life you carried, you're acknowledging that this beautiful gift from God is something to be savoured—no matter the length of time you spend together. As we remember, we invite those around us to share in the depth of love we've built for this child. We tell the world that this life is important and that this baby is gone but still oh-so-loved.

Let's remember together.

Journaling Prompts

Acts of Remembrance

- List out any activities that you would like to do in remembrance of your little one. What are some things that you think your spouse (or children) would enjoy doing? Are there any dates on which you would like to spend time in specific acts of remembrance?

- If you were to spend an entire day by yourself, reflecting on your grief and remembering your baby, what would that look like? What do you need to do to make that happen?

- Do you feel God calling you to speak out about your loss? (It may not be in the way you think.) Pray into ways that you can partner alongside other loss families within your church community. Maybe God is asking you to join a grief support group, set-up an online gathering, or share your baby's story on social media. Whatever He's asking of you, no matter your gifts and talents, begin praying for ways to partner alongside other grieving families. As you do this, journal through any thoughts, ideas, or emotions that arise.

Chapter Twelve
Feeling Alone

After my birth of my twins, I spent a week in the hospital recovering from my caesarean. It felt as if I'd been tossed overboard and left to drown in the middle of the ocean, the boat steaming off against the horizon. My lungs were filling with salt water, and it was so hard to keep my head above the waves. I was physically and emotionally depleted, and soon I began to taste the feelings of isolation that frequently arrive alongside grief.

With the exception of my husband, my parents, and my siblings, my hospital room remained void of visitors. I didn't want to see anyone. I wanted nothing more than to curl up into a blue-gowned ball and wallow in my tears. I couldn't bear to let anyone in on the intimacy of my grief; it was too raw and personal to let anyone touch the inner extent of my pain. We were extremely selective with who we let visit us in the hospital, and it was a week before we even felt strong enough to make a "public" Facebook birth announcement.

After that, it was radio silence for another six weeks until we brought our surviving twin home from the hospital. I needed time to grieve and cry on my own. I needed space to figure out the waves of emotion that I was battling minute by minute. I directed all my time and attention towards my family and my pain, and there was no room for anyone or anything else. If I was going to avoid drowning in this sea of grief, I needed to prioritize my energy.

Having time by yourself to grieve is important. Most of us are not public, community mourners. Most of us sleep on tear-stained pillows and sob our way through showers, our tears muffled and hidden. We prefer to wail through our pain in a place where no one can hear us, and this is not a bad thing in and of itself. It's important to be introspective and to look at your emotions and feelings. (This is one of the reasons why we're *journaling* together, after all!) It's good to give yourself time to grieve and process your own thoughts. We need alone time to get away from the distractions and noises of the world around us. While we know that others mean well, it's often difficult to let yourself truly and completely grieve in the presence of someone else.

With time, though, we learn that while we enjoy the space to grieve privately, we also long for the companionship and support that comes from others. If we spend too much time in isolation, we can allow feelings of loneliness and self-pity to begin to take root.

Fellow mom Lindsay says, "I have tried not to make myself isolated by talking about my losses. However, as time passes, I find myself talking about them less and less. I feel that I don't 'deserve' to talk about them. I feel like other people probably don't care to hear about it anymore, and I don't want to throw myself a pity party by continuing to bring it up. This makes me feel alone in my grief. Others have moved on, and I haven't completely."

There are many reasons why we may isolate ourselves in our grief: we may not have solid friendships or family members to lean on, or, like Lindsay, we may not feel worthy of continued support. But grief is a heavy burden to bear by ourselves. We long for the kind of supportive, listening friendships found in the movies, but not all of us have that. After a loss, friends who were once prominent in your life may begin to fade quietly into the background, or friends who were simply acquaintances may begin to grow into something much more. Seemingly overnight, the person we are and the way we view life has grown and begun to morph our priorities. The way we relate to others looks different, and these changes can either strengthen or take a toll on your relationships—not all friendships can keep up with this growth.

Joy says, "Some of my friendships have gotten stronger through this, and others have totally disappointed me by disappearing. At this point, though, I've realized that if they can't stand by me through my loss, I don't want them in my life."

Scripture speaks a lot about the importance of living life together in community and about caring for orphans and widows,[20] the poor, and the

---

20 James 1:27.

needy. We don't like to think about ourselves as someone in need. We don't like to feel "indebted" to those who support us, but these provisions have actually been put in place for us by our heavenly Father. One of the ways God provides for His children physically during a time of need is through others. The selfless act of giving and loving one another isn't something done out of requirement but out of deep love and respect for God. We lean on others, knowing that we too are called upon to lovingly offer support to others.

Ecclesiastes 4:9–12 says:

Two are better than one, because they have a good return for their labour: If either of them falls down, one can help the other up. But pity anyone who falls and has no one to help them up. Also, if two lie down together, they will keep warm. But how can one keep warm alone? Though one may be overpowered, two can defend themselves. A cord of three strands is not quickly broken. (NIV)

You've probably heard these verses shared at a wedding. While it's a beautiful analogy for marriage, it's also a great insight into community and relationship in general. For me, one line in particular jumps out from amongst these verses: *"Pity anyone who falls and has no one to help them up."* How true that is! It's so easy to fall, and to fall *hard*, after the loss of a child. It's devastating and heartbreaking, and you feel as if your world is coming to an end. You see a mother pushing her kid in the bucket-swing at the park and wonder if she's ever felt this way. You wonder why certain friends haven't asked you to hang out lately, or why those colleagues at work seem to be avoiding your Kleenex-covered desk. Perhaps you've been busy pushing people away, only to realize that they're no longer pushing back. No one seems to understand what you're going through. People are hesitant to talk about your pain, so they flit around the subject, never really allowing you to express what you feel. How can you get through this by yourself? How can you find someone to help you up and walk alongside you?

As a grieving parent, I want to offer to you three key places to find support:

1. Your Faith Community

I don't know where you are in your walk with faith. I don't know if you're a regular church attendee, or if you usually curb your visits to holidays. I don't know if your Bible is collecting dust on your shelf or if you're carrying it in your hand right now. Maybe you're new to this whole "Christianity" thing, or maybe you've loved and professed faith in God since you were a toddler. This relationship with Christ is between you and God, and only you can honestly say where you stand before Him. But no matter where you are in your faith, I encourage you to find a loving church that's passionate about God's Word and hungrily seeking Him. Find a home church where you feel comfortable asking questions, where you're free to wrestle with God's Word, and where the spiritual leaders will point you to God's truth.

It's okay if no one in the church knows that you've experienced a loss, but it *will* help if you feel comfortable opening up to someone (a small group leader, a pastor, an elder in the church, etc.). Carla shares how, after her miscarriage, she forged a spiritual mentorship with her pastor's wife, and how beneficial that was for her: "The pastor's wife helped me to identify what I was feeling (anger, sadness, loneliness, grief, anxiety, etc.), and then I located passages in the Bible that spoke to those feelings. I copied all of the passages I found into a notebook, and I refer to that notebook from time to time. Even though I was angry with God, the only thing that truly helped me was reading His Word and letting that speak truth to my heart."

Don't be afraid to contact your pastor and let him know what your family is going through. Your church should be more than willing to walk alongside you. They may be able to provide counselling, help with funeral services, make meals, pray for you, or connect you with other grieving families. The church is often the best option for extensive support during difficult times.

During the early stages of our third miscarriage, I made the conscious and purposeful decision to be upfront and open about our loss. Seated at the hospital, no firm answers in hand, I typed out a quick Facebook update asking for prayers. I asked my friends and family to believe alongside me for a miracle, but I also asked that they would pray for us to see God's faithfulness, strength, and peace at work over our lives during this difficult time.

That Sunday morning, I made my way to church feeling tired but at peace. I was reeling from the prospect of this new loss (we wouldn't receive official confirmation until the next day), and in my uncertainty, I needed to be surrounded by the body of believers. From the moment I stepped through the wooden front doors, the support I received that morning was overwhelming. I cried my way through a dozen hugs and conversations, through the worship, bits of the sermon, and the communion—but I was in a place safe enough to do that. More than any previous loss, I felt the prayers of my brothers and sisters surrounding and lifting me; I felt their encouragement, and I felt their support.

My friend Katherine shares similar feelings after her first-trimester miscarriage: "In the early days of loss, I really desired to be able to move on quickly. I had counselling, talked so much about it with those closes to me, journaled, and prayed. I returned to work soon after it happened but found that there were days when I just couldn't focus and would end up leaving work early. When I thought I was making progress, I would encounter triggers that would set me off, and I'd feel discouraged that I hadn't moved on as quickly as I'd hoped. Choosing not to isolate myself didn't come naturally, but it helped to minimize the focus on myself; I needed this not only to avoid sinking into self-pity but also to continue being involved in the lives of others. Continuing to meet with friends for prayer and Bible reading was *so* good for my soul."

Katherine explains that she felt a special closeness to God during this time. After seven months of trying to conceive, the news that they were pregnant came as a surprise. "It was an answer to prayer ... or so we thought," she says. "Two weeks later, however, we traded such joy for sorrow when we learned we were miscarrying. The grief that ensued was painful. Having other people walk with us during this time has been foundational in overcoming this dark season, especially when I felt the urge to isolate myself and give in to self-indulgence. I needed to be reminded of God's goodness. The more I shared with those closest to me, the more I felt the love and support and their prayers. I found that there was greater openness, honesty, and depth in our faith community, and most of my support came from there."

Katherine has hit upon a beautiful truth: while it's true that the church isn't perfect, we should be able to find the freedom to come before our faith community and the heavenly Father, just as we are. While it may be difficult, try to make an effort to be at church on Sunday. Everyone will understand if you need to take a few weeks off to mentally and physically recover—take the time you need! But at the same time, if you begin to find yourself purposefully avoiding church, sit down and figure out why you're feeling this way. Are you mad at God? At the other families in the church who have healthy babies? Do you feel unable to relate? Or does it just feel awkward? Don't abandon God in your pain. It's okay if it hurts too much to worship—just listen. It's okay if it hurts too much to pray—just sit in God's presence. It's okay if it hurts too much to socialize and laugh after the service—just know that these fellow believers will be there for you when you need them. It's okay if you're angry and hurt—just come with an open heart and be willing to receive.

2. Grief Community

After my first loss, the one other family who I knew had experienced the death of a child lived thousands of kilometres away. I felt alone in my grief, unable to connect with other mothers. Adding to the complexity was the fact that I'd lost one twin, while my other son was still alive. I didn't know how to navigate the great heights and depths of these conflicting emotions. That's when I booted up my computer and started searching for online twins groups. It wasn't long before I stumbled across a group of mothers who had all experienced the same diagnosis (twin-to-twin transfusion) that my boys' had. Suddenly I could connect with families who understood what I was going through. They had been through the deepest pain, yet they were still standing, still fighting. I knew then that I'd be still standing at the end too.

So many of the moms I've talked with have expressed the same thing: the power of finding community online. Emily says, "The most isolating thing about loss is that I am grieving children that no one else in the world is grieving. Everyone else just feels bad for me. When you lose someone who has lived a life, then you have others to share your grief with, others to swap memories with. When you lose your unborn babies, you're the only person who came close to knowing them. I found my community online, on

Facebook mostly, alongside other women who experienced a similar loss. Being in grief support groups specific to my experience was incredibly helpful."

Depending on where you live, it may be difficult to find opportunities to connect with other local, grieving mothers. You may have difficulty finding parents who have experienced the same diagnosis as you, lost a child in the same trimester as you, or gone through the same traumatizing experience. But in today's rapidly evolving world of social media, I guarantee that there's a Facebook group or Instagram page out there for you (and if there isn't, start one up—someone else is looking for it too).

It's also important to note that while the internet has certainly changed the face of grief, it isn't the end all and be all. Face to face conversations are important too! Book an appointment with a grief counsellor, Google search for "grieving families support groups" in your area, or invite another grieving mom out for coffee and discussion. When you're feeling alone, earnestly seek opportunities to connect with others. If you can't find a group specifically relating to pregnancy loss, join a general grief share group. This network will provide a foothold for your grief. You are not alone; there are other families who are undergoing a similar loss. Partner with them and walk alongside them. Your loss is valid and worthy of in-depth exploration, so don't be afraid to fight for personal grief connections.

3. Friends and Family

If you pull up the list of "recent contacts" on my phone, you'll find the same few numbers repeated over and over again. These are the friends and family members I call on both my worst and best days. These few numbers hear it all: my heartfelt cries, "witty" banter, deep conversations, and casual chats. So when I found myself miscarrying on the sterile sheets of a hospital bed, it was no surprise that they were the ones on the receiving end of my first calls.

During my first miscarriage, my dad volunteered to watch our two-year-old for the day while my husband and I slept off the after-effects of an anxious night spent in the ER. Later that evening, he barbequed a steak dinner, tossed a salad, and let us relax. He knew we needed someone to take care of us for a while.

Similarly, after the birth of our twins, my parents were the ones who arrived at the hospital bearing sandwiches and burgers, a fresh change of clothes, and a new toothbrush. They checked on us daily, offering up a collection of bedside prayers and shoulders to cry on. We knew our little NICU baby was well loved by the worn path that led to his incubator. When we couldn't fully function on our own, they were there to fill in any gaps.

Our friends and family are often our best check to have in place during loss. Not only do they provide much-needed support, but they're also familiar with your personality and personal history. If your grief is starting to evolve into something harmful or dangerous, these are the individuals best equipped to spot the warning signs. Postpartum depression isn't something we talk about very often after a miscarriage or stillbirth (usually we associate it with live births), but as we've heard throughout this book, it can be just as present after pregnancy loss too.

It can be challenging to know when our grief slips into depression, or when our pain becomes something more. My beautiful friend, Sandra, shares another glimpse into the resulting trauma that can take root after a miscarriage: "After we lost the baby at twelve weeks, I became a recluse and hated the sight of myself. I had, and still have, nightmares about the experience," she says. Throughout her first pregnancy, Sandra says that it just never felt "right."

One evening after a very thick discharge, Sandra and her husband headed to the hospital to be told the news that she already knew. "They told us to book a D&C and that I would experience heavy period-like bleeding in the next few days. Broken-hearted and empty, we went home and waited."

That night, Sandra awoke to a flood of blood and rushed to the bathroom. She sat bleeding for what felt like hours, but the blood wouldn't stop. Dizzy and tired, she tried to shower but ended up passing out and returned to the toilet. "I passed out again and my face went gray. My mom had my husband call an ambulance, and I was taken to the hospital," Sandra says. "I remember apologizing to the EMTs for bleeding on their bed sheets. In the ambulance, I almost passed out again, and I screamed because I thought I was dying."

In the hospital, the bleeding continued, and the tiny room swirled with staff. Sandra's husband stood terrified in the corner while she was taken to the ER and given a D&C.

"The next morning, I went home. And that was it. It was over."

Except that it wasn't fully over, as Sandra began to struggle with postpartum depression. "The feeling of losing consciousness and worrying that you might not wake up is something I will never forget," she says, "I hated myself. I couldn't sleep; I had nightmares all the time, crippling panic attacks, and uncontrollable crying. My postpartum continued this way through my next two pregnancies and has only gotten under control through the use of medication."

For Sandra, there wasn't a lot of support outside of her husband or immediate family, but the support that she did have was key: "My husband was my rock and carried me through any times when I wasn't strong enough. My family is also very open and understanding, and I never felt like I had to hide anything from them. Eventually, as we grew in community at church, I was able to speak openly about my miscarriage, and I connected with so many women who resonated with my story."

Sandra says that embracing your grief empowers you to live beyond it and with it. "Time doesn't heal wounds, but it builds wounds into something else. It's so important to let go and feel things as deeply as you need to feel them. Running from your grief is dangerous and can make it harder to live through. I would encourage anyone going through a painful loss not to hide and to never feel ashamed for feeling the way you do."

Sandra is so very right about this. It's much better to let the light shine upon our loss than to try and hide it away. We all struggle with asking for help. Weakness isn't seen as an attractive attribute, so we try to bury it. We tell ourselves that we can "handle it on our own" and that we don't need help. But this is not a truth founded in the gospel. We're not asked to carry our burdens alone.

One of my favourite stories (and an altogether beautiful picture of what it means to hold one another up) is found in Exodus 17. In this chapter, Joshua and the Israelites are battling against the Amalekites while Moses, Aaron, and Hur are standing and watching from on top of a high hill. It's then that God asks Moses to do something a little different—He asks him to hold his arms up. Just as He had done time and time again, God was going to rescue and sustain Israel, and He was going to do it in a way that demonstrated His power and purpose. Whenever Moses held up his hands, Israel began to prevail in battle, but whenever Moses lowered his hands, Amalek prevailed.

> *But Moses' hands grew weary, so they took a stone and put it under him, and he sat on it, while Aaron and Hur held up his hands, one on one side, and the other on the other side. So his hands were steady until the going down of the sun. And Joshua overwhelmed Amalek and his people with the sword.*
> —Exodus 17:12–13

This wasn't the first time God had asked Moses to raise his staff as a symbol of His divine intervention and faithfulness. But this time, Moses was physically unable to hold the weight of his task; he was unable to hold his hands up without failing. He needed help.

God didn't ask Moses to stand on his own, and He doesn't ask us to do it either. When you find your outstretched hands growing weary, begin to lean on the faith and arms of the saints around you. Standing alongside us in support, these friends and family members are pointing and directing our eyes back to the God who rescues and sustains. And in turn, when we are called to stand alongside them, we are asked to do the same.

There's no pride to be found in our self-made attempts at strength. There's no "brave face" to be put on as we approach the throne of God. We serve a big-picture God who sees us in our momentary pain and affliction and ushers us towards an everlasting hope that does not fade or wither. We serve a God who gives strength to the weary[21] and refreshes those who languish.[22] In this time of exhaustion and pain, isolation and loneliness, take advantage of the help offered. Find a community of believers and friends who will hold your arms and remind you to continue tilting your face heavenward. You don't have to battle on your own.

---

21 Isaiah 40:29.

22 Jeremiah 31:25.

Journaling Prompts

Who Are You Leaning On?

- What prevents you from asking for help? Do you ever feel embarrassed, awkward, or weak when you discuss your grief?

- Who do you think understands your grief best? Who can you really open up to about what you're going through? Have you considered talking with a professional counsellor? Why or why not?

- What do you think is the difference between loneliness and grieving alone? Are they separate or do they walk hand in hand for you? What has been the loneliest part of this loss?

Chapter Thirteen

Gratefulness in Support

Sitting cross-legged on the floor, I dumped the contents of my jewellery box out beside me and began to sort through the tangled pieces. Most of the necklaces had weaved themselves together into an elaborate braid, and sorting them out felt much like my own process with grief—a never-ending jumble of intricate twists and turns. I held a delicate necklace up against the light and watched two tiny baby birds sway on a silver branch. This pendant had been buried in a drawer for over a year, yet my heart beat a little faster at the site of it. It seemed that no matter where I turned, I came across unexpected reminders of the babies I'd lost.

It had been an incredibly thoughtful gesture. A friend had pressed the small necklace into my hand shortly after my son's funeral: a visual reminder of a heart that would always carry *two* boys. But in the chaos of the following months, the necklace was somehow designated to a box full of bent earrings and old bobby pins. A year later, as I slipped the necklace around my neck, I wondered how I could have glossed over such a beautiful gesture. Was my grief so strong and so blinding that I had been immune to friends and family who had reached out to help? I wore the necklace for the rest of the day and quietly began to wonder how many other acts of love I'd left unacknowledged in my grief. How many times had I accepted support from someone without even realizing they'd given it?

In the last chapter, we sat down and walked through *where* we find support after a loss. In this chapter, we're going to dive into that a little deeper and take a look at *what* that support might actually look like and how we respond. What do we do when our core support groups (friends, family, and our faith community) *don't* step up to help? What happens when we open ourselves up in vulnerability and get nothing in return? How do we go about asking for support in a way that will actually be beneficial?

We've discussed how many families feel isolated after loss, but adding to the complexity is the fact that our "support teams" are often just as blindsided by grief. Many times they don't know *how* to reach out, and in our grief, we often mistake this lack of support as a lack of caring.

After the loss of our firstborn son, my husband and I felt ignored by a vast majority of the community around us. We wondered why we were receiving meals from people we had never met but not from our church community. We wondered why we had been left on our own, and we questioned whether anyone really understood what we were going through. It wasn't until a year later that I finally got to the point where I could see the little acts of love and support that had previously gone unnoticed. I had been so blinded by tears that I couldn't see the vast number of supporters who were actually standing by our side. Not everyone is brave enough to intentionally wade into a world grief, yet we soon found ourselves surrounded by a network of friends, family members, acquaintances, and strangers who went out of their way to give, love, and encourage us in a time of fragility. Each of them loved us in their own way and their own time.

A year after my son's funeral, I finally sat down and wrote a letter to all those who had supported us throughout the past twelve months. (I've included a copy of the letter at the end of this chapter.) Racking my brain, I listed every possible example of support that we had received. By writing out this "letter of thankfulness," I quickly learned four key things:

1. It Helped Me to See That I Wasn't Alone

It's one thing to *know* that we're not alone, but it's another to actually see it written out before your eyes, to hold that paper in your hand and be able to point to tangible examples of support. Grief can blind us to those around us. We can feel isolated when in fact we're surrounded by individuals who love us. During the tough days, it was nice to be able to re-read through my list and remember that although the lies of the enemy whispered that I was doing this on my own, I was really surrounded by supporters.

2. It Encouraged and Developed a Supportive Community

It can be intimidating for people to actually step out and give support. Gestures that seem small to us may have taken an incredible step of bravery from the individual giving it. Taking the time to thank friends and family for their help is one way to give them helpful feedback. It acknowledges their offerings of love and time while encouraging them to continue stepping bravely forward in support of other grieving families too.

3. It Reminded Me to *Ask* for Help

It can be just as intimidating to ask for help as it is to give it. I can probably count on one hand the number of people from whom I explicitly requested help. It's not that my family didn't need help … it's just that we just didn't know *who* to ask.

The same is true in reverse. Most people are *willing* to help but they just don't know how. I can't tell you the number of times we heard someone say, "If there's *anything* I can do to help, please let me know!"

I can, however, tell you the number of times we took someone up on that offer: a big, fat, zero. While well intentioned, this is an incredibly frustrating way to offer help, as most families in the midst of grief don't even *know* what they need. When you say "anything," what *exactly* does that mean? Are you willing to clean my house? Pay my rent for the month? Make meals? Drive me to doctors' appointments? Walk my dog? It's difficult to admit that we need help and that we don't have it all under control, but it's not a bad thing to lean on someone else while you're down. When you hear someone offer to do "anything," take them up on this and accept their help! If you have a specific need, share it. Friends and acquaintances who truly want to support you will be more than happy to have a concrete way to help.

Sometimes, all you need is for someone to just *be* there. Elizabeth's story is just one of many beautiful examples of what comes from someone just taking the time to be present in your grief: encouragement and support. When Elizabeth's daughter, June Rose, came into the world, she arrived with the kicking of her big feet. But born at just eighteen-and-a-half weeks, and eight inches long, she didn't survive.

When Elizabeth's husband returned to work a week after the death of their daughter, Elizabeth felt very alone. "I had no idea how I was going to survive the day on my own without him. Not wanting to worry him more, I texted my mom and said, 'I can't do this without him.' She responded, 'You can and you will,' and then encouraged me to open my Bible and sit with God's Word." This was all the encouragement that Elizabeth needed at that moment: someone to simply be there for her when she needed help.

Elizabeth says, "I don't remember what I read that day, but I spent hours sitting at my kitchen table, sobbing and asking the Lord to help me through. I've always known that God will see me through, but ever since then, whenever things get even the slightest bit difficult, I open my Bible, read His Word, and find solitude."

Sometimes all we need from those around us are little reminders and encouragements like this, a text message that says, "You can do this. I'm here with you." And as great as it is to have people step up without us asking for it, sometimes *we* have to be the ones to take the first step. Sometimes we have to pick up our phone and shoot out a text saying, "I'm having a bad day. I need help." As daunting as it may be, don't hesitate to send an email, call a friend, or update your Facebook status. Be as open as you can about what exactly you're needing help with.

4. It Fostered an Attitude of Gratitude

Voicing my gratitude was an important step in my grieving process. I needed to show our supporters just how much I appreciated the love they'd shown me and my family. I needed them to know just how much I'd valued their help, and I wanted them to feel encouraged to help other grieving families. But more than that, it reminded *me* to be continually grateful, no matter the circumstances.

While you're in pain, it can be difficult to cultivate gratefulness. Weighed down by loss, we may struggle to see past the heavy clouds and darkening fog. This isn't to say it's impossible (I know several grieving families whose beautiful hearts and constant gratefulness inspire me daily), but it would be a lie to say that this isn't something most of us struggle with. While many of us find ourselves leaning towards passivity, scriptures show us that giving thanks to God is a fitting response to times of tribulations or trials: *"give thanks in all circumstances; for this is the will of God in Christ Jesus for you"* (1 Thessalonians 5:18).

It's not always easy to focus on what we *do have* when our hearts are crying out for a missing child. Finding things to be thankful for reminds us that there is more to life than the black hole we're currently sitting in— there is still *goodness* to be found in spite of our current circumstances. You may not yet be able to see anything to be grateful for, and that's okay. Find simple things and start there. Sometimes this means whispers of gratefulness for hot showers, a steaming cup of coffee, or the minty flavour of freshly-cleaned teeth. Be thankful in a car that makes it to the station without running out of gas, in the beams of sunshine that dance across kitchen floors, or in the easily overlooked fact that we woke up this morning. Slowing down and looking for God's gifts throughout the day helps direct our constant attention back to Him. Finding thankfulness in our everyday activities reminds us that although our world has been changed, God is unchanging. His faithfulness remains the same.

One of those grieving mamas whose story inspires me to live with a grateful heart is Cassie. After the death of her daughter, Cassie says that she was incredibly blessed by the friends and family members who stepped up. She writes, "I never expected to be so supported by people outside of our immediate family. Friends I'd lost touch with over the years have sent me cards and let me know through emails and Facebook messages that they are constantly thinking of us and praying for us. It has been such an encouragement to me, and I know that God has placed these people in my life for a reason: friends who didn't hesitate to come at the drop of a hat, or family who booked last minute flights to be with us. How can I explain the number of blessings we received without giving God the credit? He has orchestrated all of this and knows just what I need."

Cassie's Story

Cassie's daughter was born still at eighteen weeks. From the beginning of her pregnancy, things had felt different, and Cassie had struggled with strange abdominal pains. Around sixteen weeks, she noticed that her legs were getting really swollen, so she began to wear compression socks to work, which never really worked. At seventeen weeks, she developed a severe headache and was in constant pain. At eighteen weeks, while at work as a nurse, her co-workers commented on how terrible and pale she looked, and they took her blood pressure. At 174/107, the fellow nurses had her book an immediate doctor's appointment, after which she was admitted into the hospital.

"After having an ultrasound the next day," Cassie says, "the doctor came in and explained to us that this was not a normal pregnancy. There was a 'mole,' or another placenta, invading my uterus. She said that my body was starting to shut down, and I would not be able to keep the baby, as it wouldn't survive in the womb, nor would I survive by keeping it and the extra 'mole' either."

Cassie was transferred to a hospital in the city where the doctors explained that she would be induced immediately, as her body was getting sicker. With her high blood pressure, the medical staff was worried that she would begin seizing. Her water broke early that morning, and after pushing for a while, the doctors transferred her to an operating room and put her under. After her body pushed the baby out, the doctor went in and removed the two placentas. Cassie says, "I delivered a beautiful baby girl. She was 136 grams and perfect. My husband and I were able to name her, hold her, and take pictures with her. The hospital gave us a certificate of life for her, along with a box of footprints and handprints, a blanket she was wrapped in, and a few other things. They had a social worker talk with us and then set us up with a funeral home so we could have her cremated."

For Cassie, being surrounded by people who genuinely cared was a huge help to her grieving process. "So many people sent us cards and flowers: my boss at work, and even the labour and delivery unit. One of my best friends wrote us a beautiful song in memory of our daughter, which meant so much to us. Also knowing that our little girl was immediately taken back into the arms of Jesus was a huge relief. We have faith that we will see her again and that she's free from the pain and darkness of this world." Despite such a difficult pregnancy, Cassie says, "I feel so grateful to have been able to carry my little girl for eighteen weeks."

Gratefulness in Support

Just listening to Cassie's story, it's evident to see her gratefulness and support ripple off the page. I know that this is an inspiration to me, and I hope it is for you too. If you're having trouble finding things to be grateful for, start by writing a letter to those who have supported you throughout this time of loss. You don't have to share this publicly, but at the same time, it might be beneficial for both you and them. Open up a blank journal page and give thanks to God for bringing these people into your life. If you're struggling with where to start, feel free to use the following letter as a template.

A Letter to Those Who Have Loved Us, Each in Their Own Way and Their Own Time

In an inadequate attempt to display the depth of my gratitude, this letter is for all those who have walked alongside us with patience, comforting arms, giving hearts, and listening ears.

Today, I simply say *thank-you*.

You know who you are. You are the few courageous souls who chose to walk this dusty road with your arms around our shoulders, braving the storm, your tears mingling with ours.

Thank you for being brave enough to act, to speak, and to comfort.

Thank you for not worrying about getting tangled in the awkwardness of grief but for choosing to love despite the mess.

You were the ones who refused to shy away from pain but instead surrounded us with fresh tissues and a listening ear, the ones who found the fine balance between giving us space and wrapping us tightly in your arms. Your visits brought laughter, yet you were brave enough to stick around for the tears.

You created a safe place for a brittle heart to open up and share its deepest pain. You reminded us that we were not alone, that you'd been *here* too, and that grief would not always be this heavy.

You were the ones brave enough to say our baby's name, to let us know that he is missed. You showed your love by decorating our home with picture frames, wooden ornaments, necklaces, artwork, and personalized Christmas stockings. You never avoided discussing but instead acknowledged and cherished his existence.

You took the time and energy to mail us care packages, books on grief, and support-filled letters. You baked us meals, made stunning flower arrangements, and helped organize a beautiful funeral. I am astounded by your generosity.

We felt your prayers and your tears from across the city and around the globe; we awoke in the night knowing that *you* were still praying. Distance was no barrier to your support.

There are no words to express our gratitude for each and every one of you. All we can say is "thank you." From the depths of our hearts, *thank you*.

I understand that this role you've played has at times been uncomfortable, but I want you to know that it's been a vital part of our journey. When our legs buckled under the weight of grief, you were part of the community that helped us find our feet.

We all know that it "takes a village to raise a child." But the opposite is true too. It takes a village to *mourn* a child. And you *chose* to be a part of our village: to mourn and to love. You didn't have to do what you've done. You didn't have to step up. But you did. And for that, we are *ever* so grateful.

Journaling Prompts

What Does Gratitude Look Like in Your Life Today?

- How has grief affected your attitude towards gratitude? Create a list of things you've been thankful for in this season. Keep your list close and add to it throughout the day.

- Write a thank you letter to someone who has supported you during this time of loss (or this could be a letter similar to the one that I wrote, addressed to your entire community of support). Write down exactly what their support means to you. If you feel comfortable, feel free to send it to them; if not, keep it for a future date to remind you of those whom you can lean on during tough days.

- Do you find it easy or difficult to ask for support? What kind of help/support do you need right now? Create a list of individuals who you think you would be willing to help you.

Chapter Fourteen

You're Still a Mom

(This chapter deals with pregnancy after loss and the challenges that may arise from that. I know that for some of you, this is an incredibly painful subject. Some of you may skip this chapter and come back to it later ... or not at all. The goal of this book is not to further wound, but to allow you to work through different aspects of your grieving process—which for many women includes thinking about or dealing with a pregnancy after loss.)

For many women, there comes a day in the grieving process when your brain starts thinking about having another child. Ignoring your heart's feeble protests, you immediately begin calculating due dates and conception dates. You may know you aren't yet ready for another pregnancy, another babe, but you can't seem to toss this newfound hope. The thought is tempting and promising, and now that it's firmly and irrevocably planted in your head, there's no way to shake it loose.

For me, that thought arrived two days after the loss of my son Landon. Lying in the hospital room in a milk-soaked pregnancy bra and stretchy maternity pants, my heart began to ache for the child I never knew. The sound of crying infants echoed down the hallway and across the ward, a reminder of my own baby's silence. My arms longed for the weight of his little body, and I knew that nothing would fill the empty hollow in my chest. I had been so intent on bringing two babies home from the hospital, I couldn't wrap my head around the fact that suddenly I was left with only one. I wanted to start trying for another child as soon as it was physically possible.

It didn't take me too long to realize that I didn't want *another* child; I wanted the one I'd just lost. In my grief, I'd confused my desire to have Landon back as a desire to have another child. But even if I had been able to get pregnant that soon, conceiving a child as a way to "replace" the one I'd lost was not a healthy idea. My head knew that grief takes time, but my heart was wildly impatient.

After my immediate initial longing for another baby, the pendulum swung hard the other way, and for the following eighteen months, the thought of getting pregnant again was nauseating. I couldn't imagine having to go through nine months of waiting, fears, and painful pregnancy symptoms. Knowing the reality of pregnancy loss, it took time for me to open my heart to the prospect of loving and carrying another little one.

Britt expresses similar feelings after the birth of her rainbow son, who was born after two first-trimester miscarriages. Britt says, "I was so terrified the entire time I was pregnant with my second son. I was so nervous that we'd lose him too. We tried again because we always wanted a second child, but I think if we'd lost a third baby, we may have just settled with the one. I couldn't go through it again. I don't want to risk losing any more." This fear of additional loss is very real in subsequent pregnancies. The naivety you carried throughout your first pregnancy has slipped through your fingers, leaving a trail of worry and anxiety in its wake.

It's hard to talk about pregnancy after loss, simply because we all have different journeys. Statistically, many mothers reading this chapter will struggle with infertility, many will face future losses and grief, and many will go on to have "normal" full-term pregnancies. Some of us will decide to try again; some will not. Some will go on to have healthy future pregnancies, while others will struggle with the same chromosomal abnormalities time and time again. Not knowing which of these categories you fit into can be nerve-wracking. But there are a few truths that I can tell you about pregnancy after loss, and while they may not be easy to hear, they are important to wrestle with:

1. Pregnancy after Loss Can Be Challenging

As I faced the prospect of another pregnancy, I had to ask myself some difficult questions. Was I ready to purposefully ask God to breathe life into my womb, all the while knowing that at any time, this new little one may be gently ushered home to Him? Was I ready to open up my heart to this pain again? Gone was the fragile assurance I had cradled throughout my first pregnancy—the ridiculous notion that because I'd made it through the first trimester, everything was going to be okay. Another pregnancy would bring with it a new type of exhaustion, a new type of awareness.

This newfound awareness and loss of naivety is something that many women experiencing a pregnancy after loss struggle with. Amy shares how terrifying her pregnancy after miscarriage was: "I started spotting after getting positive bloodwork back, and I went to the doctor right away. She said there was nothing she could do so just wait it out. The bleeding did stop and I went on to carry my baby to term, but every time I went to the bathroom I'd check to see if I was bleeding. I spent months constantly waiting to miscarry again."

Marina echoes a similar sentiment: "My third pregnancy was very difficult both physically and emotionally. I faced constant fear that my baby was not going to make it, and I was afraid to celebrate or enjoy my pregnancy." Marina had reason to worry about this. At nineteen weeks her placenta had begun to separate, and she experienced second-trimester bleeding. "I was at risk for pre-term labour. All I could do was pray that this little one would make it."

Marina's previous pregnancy had ended in a six-week loss. Having had a positive pregnancy test a week earlier, Marina purchased an additional digital test to photograph and mark the beginning of her second pregnancy. "For some reason, this test showed that I was only one to two weeks pregnant," she says. "I immediately thought that something was wrong, but when my husband and I googled this, it said that the test could simply be defective." Three days later, Marina awoke to light spotting. While driving to work, she started to bleed heavier and headed straight to the hospital. The ultrasound confirmed that the pregnancy and the life of her sweet little one was over. When Marina became pregnant again after this miscarriage, it wasn't easy. She shares, "Pregnancy after loss is full of fear, and a new pregnancy never substitutes for the baby that is gone. I wish people would know that we didn't try for a new pregnancy to forget our miscarriage; we tried because we still wanted to expand our family."

Fear is a completely normal reaction to loss. It can be frightening to think of what *may* happen, especially when you have a deeper understanding of potential risks. The important thing is to not let the fear of loss rob you of the opportunity to love another little one. Loss hurts because we loved, but wouldn't we rather love too much than too little? We cannot tell what size or shape our family will take in the future, what heartbreaks we will face, or what mountains we will conquer. In an already emotional time, the fear of the unknown can cause additional anxiety and stress. If we let it, this fear can bind us and tie us, preventing us from moving forward. But despite the vast depth of our worries, there is a God whose promised freedom runs so much deeper.

This doesn't mean that we won't experience anxiety or have bad days. Life after loss can be messy and painful. It won't be all butterflies and rainbows. It won't "fix" your grief or fill the empty spots in your heart. When thinking about whether or not you're ready to have another child, examine your grief and your motivation. Don't hold back from another pregnancy on account of fear, but as Marina shared earlier, don't rush into it as a way to try to ease your pain.

When I discovered I was pregnant for the third time, I was excited and understandably nervous. I'd miscarried less than three months earlier, and the pain was still very fresh. I wondered how many pregnancies I'd be able to go through before it became too much to handle. How many babies would I have to hold in my heart alone? While I was ready for this opportunity to carry another life, I also knew that having to say a premature goodbye was a very real possibility.

Right from the start, that pregnancy was fraught with complications and endless waiting. I came home from the doctor's office expecting to have had my pregnancy confirmed and instead was sent for a round of bloodwork, and then another. The memories from the past three months came flooding back, and I began to feel frustrated, crying out, "God, haven't I lost enough?"

And then I heard something that I will cling to throughout all my future pregnancies. A gentle voice whispered to my heart, saying, "I have given you this baby not that you might live in fear, but that you may glorify Me in the midst of uncertainty."

In that moment, I made a decision. I was not going to let my days with this little one be dominated by anxiety. No matter the length of time

I had with this baby, I was going to cherish each and every day. I was going to celebrate their life for as long as they had it, and wake up each morning with praise and thanksgiving on my lips. And when that pregnancy ended at eleven weeks, I knew that I had done my best with the gift I'd been given.

Only you will know when the timing is right to try for another baby. You know your heart and the grief it's working through. Allow yourself time to process your loss before trying to conceive again. As painful as it may be to wait, it will be more painful if you begin trying again before you're ready. Mandy shares a little bit about this when she says, "I was so desperate to be pregnant again, but I didn't realize how stressful a rainbow pregnancy would be. I wanted another child so badly, but I should have waited. I should have given myself more time to heal."

Pregnancy hormones take a toll on any woman's emotions, but after a loss, this additional stress may stir up a whole new level of anxiety and questions. Jessica shares how the pregnancy and birth of her rainbow daughter actually stirred up *more* fears and grief than in the months initially following her miscarriage. "I experienced anxiety and panic attacks after my rainbow daughter was born," Jessica says. "I would just look at her and grieve the fact that I didn't get to experience these milestones with my first. I would study her features and wonder if my son would have looked like her."

These sorts of thoughts and feelings are completely normal, not only during a pregnancy after loss, but also prior to a rainbow's conception or after their birth. As Kristy considers another pregnancy, she says, "The fear of another loss is very great, but maybe greater than that is the fear that my son will be forgotten by myself or by others. I worry about people forgetting the reality of my grief once there's another baby in my arms. And I worry about being reminded of all that I missed with my son as I watch another child grow up." As you prayerfully consider growing your family, begin emotionally preparing yourself to deal with similar thoughts or questions. They may arise in different forms, or not at all, but by equipping yourself in advance, you'll be better prepared to analyze and recognize what you're feeling.

Most of all, remember to be patient with yourself and take this one day at a time. As you prepare to become pregnant again, and as you walk through your next pregnancy, intentionally cling to the peace that can only come from above. John 14:27 says, *"Peace I leave with you; my peace I give to you. Not as the world gives do I give to you. Let not your hearts be troubled, neither let them be afraid."*

It's natural for the fears to creep in, and I know that they won't disappear simply by telling ourselves not to be afraid. But as these fears rise, I encourage you to hold fast to the reassurance that our victory in Christ has already been won. There are no guarantees that your pregnancy will be easy, but there is the guarantee of a God upon whom we can lean. These momentary, earthly battles that we currently fight will one day pass away. No matter the days ahead, there is a God who promises to walk this road alongside us. Whether you encounter this pain once, twice, or a hundred times, He will remain with us in the pain and muck. He is with us. He will hold our families in His hands, just as He holds our babies in His arms: *"Have I not commanded you? Be strong and courageous. Do not be frightened, and do not be dismayed, for the Lord your God is with you wherever you go"* (Joshua 1:9).

2. You May Never Have Another Child

People around you may have tried to comfort you with the frustratingly false reassurance that, "You can always have another child." (Don't even get me started on the oh-so-many things wrong with this statement!) But the honest and painful truth is that this sentiment isn't always true. For some of us, even talking about another pregnancy is painful and raw. It may have been difficult, even excruciatingly so, to get pregnant the first time. Losing this baby may have felt as if you were watching all your hopes and dreams swirl quietly and quickly down the drain. You may worry that you'll never be able to get pregnant again, or you may already *know* that you'll never be able to carry another child. Even for those whose last pregnancy came about easily, a healthy child is no guarantee.

After my stillbirth, I heard "reassuring" comments like, "Well, since this was solely a twin thing, you don't have to worry about losing any future pregnancies." I quickly learned that while these hollow promises sounded comforting, they rang with false reassurances and blatant lies. Life isn't a game of Monopoly: you can't simply pull a "get out of jail free card" and promise me that I'll get to keep all my babies. When it comes to pregnancy, we do not have ultimate control over the outcome.

These same comments began to pop up after my first and second miscarriages. The emergency room doctors assured me that it was very rare to have two miscarriages in a row. Statistics say that just 2 per cent of women will experience two miscarriages in a row, while only 1 per cent of women experience three or more consecutive losses.[23] Unfortunately for me and countless other women around the globe, some of us will end up being those "rare" statistics.

It's important to remain realistic (without veering into debilitating fear) about the possibility of future loss or infertility. There's no guarantee that we will have another child. Some mothers lose infant after infant after infant. Our heart breaks time and time again as these promises and optimism melt into meaningless, untrustworthy drivel. As these assurances dissolve before our eyes, we begin to grieve more than the baby we lost in miscarriage or stillbirth—we begin to grieve the future children we had hoped for.

Scripture is full of stories about barren women who had their wombs opened and who became pregnant or delivered children in miraculous ways: Sarah (Genesis 18:9–15), Rachel (Genesis 30:22), Hannah (1 Samuel 1), and Elizabeth (Luke 1), just to name a few. None of these stories speak direct promises over our lives. None of them guarantee that our story will have the same supernatural outcome. But at the same time, they do give us a glimpse into the agony, heartache, and anguish that comes with infertility. They remind us that it's okay to mourn an empty womb and to prayerfully ask God to fill it. These women's stories remind us that God has not forgotten the pain that comes with barrenness and points us to the goodness of God's great plan. I encourage you to spend some time in God's Word, studying the stories of these women—not as a promise of future pregnancy, but as a way to see God at work amidst the heartache of our stories too.

Regardless of whether our house is brimming with children or not, our stories are still good—for no other reason than simply because they belong to God. Even our story's soggiest, most tear-stained pages have been written by a faithful and just God who sees what we cannot. A God

---

23 "5 Things You Should Know About Recurrent Miscarriages," USCFertility, accessed on August 13, 2019, http://uscfertility.org/5-things-know-recurrent-miscarriages/.

who steadfastly walks beside us in our darkest days and says, "I hear your prayers, I see your heartache, and I am here." Even here, God is at work! On this side of Heaven, we cannot see the fullness of God's story or the work that is being done, yet we can trust that because it belongs to Him, it *is* good. It can be easy to make these stories of infertility and loss about us, to focus ourselves inwards rather than upwards, but I pray that as we walk through these difficult, uncertain days, Christ will be glorified evermore.

Thinking of this, I'm reminded of the story of a fellow grieving mother, Dulci. When I first heard her story, I was immediately touched by her son's name: Samuel. It was clear that after the loss of her son, Dulci had found herself reflecting on the biblical story of Hannah, and I found that to be extraordinarily beautiful. Even in their deepest pain, these parents chose to acknowledge the fact that their son did not belong to them but that he belonged to the heavenly Father who had given him life. The recognized that the story God had given them was about *something more*, and they chose to glorify Him with the life of their son.

Dulci's Story

Dulci and her husband had just bought their dream farm when they were surprised by a fourth pregnancy. Their new home was more rural and less comfortable, and with three kids and a house to sell, the thought of adding a new baby into the mix seemed overwhelming. Placing their ultimate trust in God, they chose to be excited about the little one growing in her womb.

The pregnancy was similar to her previous three, with the exception that this time around, Dulci's body seemed to be wearing out. The sciatica that bothered her somewhat with her first child was almost crippling with the fourth. With the back pain, a new property that was demanding their attention, and a toddler who still needed to be occasionally carried, it was going to be a long pregnancy.

But not as long as they'd thought. At exactly twenty-one weeks, Dulci and her husband went in for a routine ultrasound. Going into the ultrasound with trepidation, Dulci tried to push back the ominous worry that had plagued her for the past two weeks. While she thought she'd felt her baby move around fourteen or fifteen weeks, she hadn't felt many (if any) kicks since nineteen weeks.

Due to some screening for a heart condition, Dulci was not surprised by the doctor who came to review her scan. Silently studying the screen for a moment, the doctor took a deep breath and said, "There's no easy way to say this, but there is no heartbeat."

When Dulci's son was born, she held his little body close—a body that measured just 9 ¾ inches. She saw his perfect toes and fingers, his nose and mouth and eyelids. Before the delivery, Dulci had feared seeing and holding him. She had wondered what two weeks of decomposition would do to a baby. Would they even know if he was a boy or girl, or would all traces of gender be gone? Would his body be born whole or mangled by all the time she had carried him without knowing he was gone?"

But God, in His graciousness, gave them a whole, complete baby boy to hold. In writing about her birth story, Dulci says, "I remember telling him how sorry I was, how I loved him. I remember feeling his full weight in my arms. I thought he would feel like a mostly deflated balloon, almost weightless, wrapped up in a blanket. But seven ounces is a weight that registers; though he was so much tinier than my full-term babies, he had substance. He existed. I held him and felt his weight."

In the days leading up to her delivery, Dulci found herself remembering the biblical character of Hannah. In 1 Samuel 1, God gives Hannah a much-desired son, and when the boy was weaned, Hannah took him and dedicated him to the service of the temple. As much as it grieved her heart to do so, Dulci knew that she needed to dedicate this child to God. So when her husband asked her if she had any ideas about what to name this child, one name quickly sprung to mind: Samuel. Her husband suggested the middle name, John. Later during Samuel's memorial service, Dulci found out that he had suggested the name as a reminder that their baby was loved by Jesus.

Dulci says that after her loss she heard insensitive comments like, "You can totally have another one! You've had three healthy babies before!" But Dulci and her husband aren't sure yet if they're waiting on a rainbow baby or if they're just done. Dulci says, "If Samuel was to be my last baby, this was an unbelievably tragic way to end my childbearing years. I don't want it to end like this, but I don't know if my husband, my body, or even my soul, can handle another pregnancy."

Sometimes our stories end here too: with uncertainty and confusion. While the world likes to tell us otherwise, not all families go on to have more children after a loss. This chapter was not written to scare you. The goal of this chapter is to bring light to an issue that's rarely talked about. It's a crushing truth that's all too real for many of us: the struggle with the heavy burden of infertility and recurrent loss. But despite the uncertainty of our futures, you now have something that no one can ever take away from you. Today, and for the rest of your life, you are and always will be someone's mother.

I know that your heart longs for your missing baby. You want the world to see that you are a mother, that your little one was *here* and that they belong to you. But even if you never hold another little one in your arms, even if you never get to rub your cheek against their downy hair and smell their sweet baby scent—*you are still a mother.* For a few days or a few months, you carried your child. A piece of your DNA was woven into theirs, and they will always belong to you. You can't see them, but they're there. They will always be a part of your heart and your life, and you will never forget them. You have been given the life-altering, permanent title of mother; you simply carry your little ones in your heart instead of your arms.

This isn't what you would have chosen for your family to look like, but God has orchestrated something different for you. That knowledge can feel painful—incredibly so. Don't be afraid to cry out to Him in your anguish. Don't be afraid to tell Him exactly how you are feeling. Even though your heart is breaking, continue to trust that He is big enough to hold this pain and to draw you nearer to Him. In Matthew 11:28–30, Jesus says:

> *Come to me, all who labour and are heavy laden, and I will give you rest. Take my yoke upon you, and learn from me, for I am gentle and lowly in heart, and you will find rest for your souls. For my yoke is easy, and my burden is light.*

These verses are for you and for me, the heavy laden. Come to Him and lay down your heavy burdens at His feet. It is in Christ that our souls find rest, refreshment, and eternal promise. And when we place our hope and trust in Him alone, we can begin to face and conquer the doubts and fears that plague us. This doesn't make trust in Christ some sort of "magic cure" for doubt, anger, or pain. Truthfully, living your life as a follower of Jesus might make things *more* difficult. But it does mean that we walk this road with the reassurance of a God who is standing beside us, one who will never abandon us, and who will one day usher us home to be in His presence for a painless, beautiful eternity.

It's okay if there are days when you struggle to believe that He is still good. It's okay if some days you don't feel like you *can* believe. We cannot do this on our own; He knows the depth of our hurt. On the days when you can't stand by yourself, turn your empty, wounded hands to Him and simply ask Him to be there. He is enough.

> *And after you have suffered a little while, the God of all grace, who has called you to his eternal glory in Christ, will himself restore, confirm, strengthen, and establish you.*
>
> —1 Peter 5:10

Journaling Prompts

What Does Motherhood Look Like to You?

- Where are you in this process? Do you long for another child? Never want to get pregnant again? Do you think these feelings will change in time? How has this loss (or losses) changed the way you look at family planning?

- What are your fears surrounding pregnancy after loss? What are some ways that you can work through these anxieties?

- If you are someone who has struggled with infertility or recurrent pregnancy loss, how much pain do you think your heart is able to hold? How much love is your heart able to hold? How do these questions affect whether or not you continue trying for a healthy pregnancy? How would you feel if God said that your family was complete as it is?

Chapter Fifteen

Leaning into Grief

We were speaking at an event for grieving families when I first heard my husband tell the small crowd that we needed to "lean into our grief." Initially, these words felt contradictory and foolish. I imagined myself leaning in and plunging over the edge, falling headlong into a black tunnel of numbness and inability. The pain was buried deep beneath the surface, and I worried that if I fully leaned into it, I'd never be able to crawl out again. The bitter sting of salty tears against open wounds wasn't exactly something I wanted to sit and revel in, but I soon realized that if I wanted to get the most out of my grief, I needed to embrace *all* that it held.

My husband's insight brought my understanding of grief to a whole new level. By leaning into our grief, we become active participants in exploring and uncovering its intricacies. We take charge of our grief story and pursue a healthier view of life after loss.

Those who chose *not* to lean into their grief are those who have decided to walk away from the pain. Blindly casting aside their tears, their grief sits stagnant and untouched, lying deep within them. They box in the gurgling emotions building within and run from their feelings of grief, casting aside anything that would bring them to a true place of restoration.

If we follow in their example, we allow ourselves to numb. We refuse to dig into our pain and hinder ourselves from even the most tentative steps forward. Grief that is undealt with will continue to fester. As we allow those feelings of numbness to permeate throughout us, we become hopeless in preventing it from touching all aspects of our life. Eventually, those feelings of lethargy and apathy begin to creep their way into our spiritual walks of faith too.

That is what this journey has been all about: leaning into our grief and uncovering our stories. With grief comes discovery and redemption. And as we begin to peel back the layers and depths of sorrow, we learn that by leaning into grief, we must simultaneously lean into Christ. We must allow Him to redeem the wretchedness of this situation in His way; in the depths of this devastation, there is still beauty to be found in Christ.

You never expect to have to bury your child in a tiny, muddy grave. You never expect to watch bits and pieces of your pregnancy circle down the toilet while you hold your head in your hands and wail for the babe you never got to hold. These are the moments that catch you unaware, they suck your breath away and force you to see the fragility of life. Everything you know can dissolve in an instant; every bit of control you once felt was simply an illusion.

When I hit this powerless place of pain and emptiness, I could not stand on my own. There was no strength left to bear this grief. The pain was excruciating: it radiated from my bones to my innermost being, and I could do nothing but weep. I wept for the children that I had lost and cried out for God to rescue me from this place of hopelessness. And it was here that I heard the still, soft whisper of a God who does not abandon His children, telling me to simply *give* it all to Him.

> *For we do not have a high priest who is unable to sympathize with our weaknesses, but one who in every respect has been tempted as we are, yet without sin. Let us then with confidence draw near to the throne of grace, that we may receive mercy and find grace to help in time of need.*
>
> —Hebrews 4:15–16

On my knees, weighted down by an inexpressible heaviness, there was nowhere else to run except to God. As I leaned into my grief, I quickly came to the realization that I could not hold it together on my own. It was impossible to carry the fragmented pieces of my life and glue them back together by myself. I needed to cling to something and someone bigger than my own opinionated plans and ideas of how life should be. And so I let go and grabbed hold of the One who was already drawing me near.

I didn't learn to embrace because it came naturally or because it was easy. I learned to embrace because I had no choice. There was no one else to lean on except Christ. There was nowhere to cling to for strength except the cross. I want you to know that we serve a God who *understands* our pain. Two thousand years ago, Jesus was nailed to a wooden cross for sins He did not commit. He died the death we should have died, so that we may know God and one day glorify Him eternally: *"For God so loved the world, that he gave his only Son, that whoever believes in him should not perish but have eternal life"* (John 3:16).

For those who mourn, there is exceeding hope to be found in the Gospels. We can face tomorrow knowing that we worship a God who has defeated death, a God who does not delight in our demise but *sent His son to die* so that we may live abundantly. If there is anyone who understands the pain of separation from those we love, it is our heavenly Father: *"The thief comes only to steal and kill and destroy. I came that they may have life and have it abundantly"* (John 10:10).

In these dark recesses of grief, frustration, and hurt, you have a choice. You can choose to struggle along on your own, or you can choose to let go and lean on Christ. This is not an easy decision: it is the act of laying all you are, all you own, and all you dream of at the foot of the cross. No matter the dark nights that lie ahead, or the suffering and brokenness that we've seen, we have to trust that God will continue to faithfully stand alongside us through the good and the bad.

I am reminded of a few simple and precious words given to me by fellow loss mama, Promise, who said, "Real faith starts when you trust anyway, not knowing the whole story."

How true this is—how limited our vision is in comparison to the omniscient God we serve. We trust blindly but not carelessly. We trust that there is more to this story than today.

Promise's story of loss isn't one that's talked about very often. In today's world, the line drawn around when life begins looks grey and fuzzy, and that can be difficult for individuals who experience a loss like Promise's. It's in Christ that we find permission to grieve the types of losses that the world deems trivial or inconsequential. In Christ, we have the freedom to embrace and recognize that our grief is valid, no matter what the shifting opinions of the world around us may proclaim.

Promise's Story

After four years of infertility and testing, Promise and her husband began IVF. After eighteen eggs were retrieved, ten of them were fertilized, but over the next week, they kept losing embryos. Promise explains, "After fertilization, embryos grow in a Petri dish for so many days on their own. When they stop growing, it's considered a loss. For us, the big day was day five, when the doctors called to tell us that none of the embryos were strong enough or growing enough to freeze but that they would give it one more day." Miraculously, the doctors called back the next day to tell Promise that two had made it.

"My heart hurt and mourned for my eight babies, but I was so happy for my fighting two. A month later we transferred those two embryos. I wasn't supposed to, but I cheated and took a test before my blood draw to confirm—it was positive!" For Promise, though, the first ultrasound became bittersweet when the doctor found the first heartbeat but not the second.

"Panic set in when I realized that the other one hadn't made it," Promise shares. "I lost complete control at that point. With my legs still up in the stirrups, the wand still probing my insides, I wailed. All the grief hit me at once and there was no stopping the floodgates. Yes, I was unbelievably grateful for one baby still growing, but my mommy heart hurt deep thinking of the nine we had lost."

Promise says that, for her, embracing grief means allowing yourself to truly feel the emotion that may come your way. And I agree. As we lean into our grief, tumbling headlong over the rails and down the damp well of pain and loss, we will eventually find ourselves hitting rock bottom. It's here we discover that without Christ, we are nothing. We cannot begin to move forward without the realization that there is more to this story than just ourselves. While our lives appear to be our whole world, we are but a minuscule drop in the bucket of God's great narrative.

So how can we continue moving forward after such loss? By acknowledging that there is more to this life than what we can see. Many grieving families get caught up in the fact that on our own, this loss is pointless. We fail to see that with Christ, we hold a testament of God's goodness and glory. With Christ, we've been given a tiny taste of the joyous, heavenly reunion that awaits us. This life is not just about us.

A few months ago, I was given the privilege of connecting with a beautiful mother named Kristy. Her story is a testimony of the grace and goodness of Christ, and of the abundance that can come with death. She says, "My loss has changed me so much. Before I lost my son, I actually feared death and Heaven. Now I fear living so much more. To have half of your heart on earth and half in Heaven is a strange phenomenon. I feel like my life has deepened with this new grasp of sorrow, and in turn I also experience life's joys in a greater way. Hearing about pain or poverty on the news crushes me in a new way, but the jokes are also funnier, the colours brighter. I had heard about God's grace and presence in the midst of great tragedy, but now I know about these things firsthand."

I love Kristy's understanding of joy and acknowledgement of God's grace in the midst of loss. Kristy went through a particularly frightening and intense birth with her son, Luther. Yet surrounded by rolling clouds of loss, her faith in God shines through as encouragement for other breaking hearts.

Kristy's Story

Kristy was thirty-nine weeks pregnant when she began to feel the first tingling of early labour, followed closely after by a sense of light-headedness and bouts of loss of consciousness. The night before had been rough, full of strong baby kicks and a bad head cold forming, so Kristy told her family not to panic. "I told them that I was sick and probably just had a stomach bug, because I was experiencing a lot of pressure in my abdomen." As Kristy's sister and husband went to help her to the bathroom, Kristy blacked out and awoke to find her sister on the phone with a 911 operator, receiving instructions as to how to deliver a baby at home.

"I recall hearing many voices in our house and being taken in an ambulance to our local hospital," she says. "I was frustrated that everyone was being so dramatic and overreacting, because I prefer to labour at home for as long as possible. Nurses began to cram into the small delivery room where I learned I was five centimetres dilated, but I was still so lightheaded that it was difficult for me to be truly aware of what was happening." Using an ultrasound machine to search Kristy's belly, the doctor told the family, with tears in her eyes, that she could not detect any heartbeat or fetal movement. "I said that I didn't understand. It felt like a dream. And then the nurse beside my head leaned over and said, 'Kristy, your baby has died.'" Kristy looked over at her husband to see tears pouring down his face. She heard her sister wailing, her mother praying, and their small-town nurses crying.

Kristy was transferred to a city hospital an hour away, and when she asked the paramedic if her husband come too, the paramedic said no. "My doctor and head delivery nurse protested at this, so my husband was able to sit up front with the driver, which was definitely against protocol. My doctor and nurse rode with me, cradling my head in their hands and giving counter pressure on my back." Kristy had suffered a complete placental abruption, and blood was pooling in her uterus, explaining her low blood pressure and abdominal pain. Kristy later learned that the strange ambulance set up was due to the fact that her doctor had thought they might lose her on the drive.

Upon arrival at the hospital, the doctors weren't able to give her anesthesia due to her unsafe blood pressure level. Eventually, the doctor said that Kristy would need to deliver her baby naturally as she had her first two sons.

"My mother is a trained doula," Kristy says, "but with no encouraging incentive to offer, the task of motivating me through the difficult pushing phase was left up to God alone. I climbed to my knees, leaning over the back of the raised bed, and pushed in a rhythm whispered to me by a private Voice. As my third son, Luther, was delivered, my physical pain was gone but a new pain had begun. The usual celebratory sounds of the delivery room were replaced with sombre silence. I was given my still son to hold; he was so beautiful and soft and smelled just as good and sweet as his two older brothers had."

This wasn't Kristy's first loss, as she had also experienced a previous miscarriage at fifteen weeks. "When I had my miscarriage with my daughter, Jael, my neighbour came over to bring flowers and cry with me. She told me that she too had lost a daughter thirty-five years ago, at full term. I remember thinking that I could never deliver a baby who had died that far along in pregnancy; I couldn't survive that kind of loss. And then, that very thing happened to me. Not only did I survive the delivery, but I have survived every day without my son since then. But not just survived—it's been so much more than that. How I wish that I could have known the far-reaching grace of God for those who suffer this loss, the tender whispers of Christ that are reserved for those who are broken by death. I wish I knew that we never have to fear our worst nightmares, because Jesus is everywhere."

I hope that Kristy's story, and the stories of all the other women that have filled these pages with their testaments of life and hope, are an encouragement to you today. At the beginning of this book, I said that I prayed you would begin to uncover the beauty found in your story. It seems impossible that anything good can bloom from the sorrow surrounding the death of a child. But in these moments of pain and anguish, we *can* find glimpses of something beautiful—we just have to know where to look. There is beauty to be found as we rediscover our complete reliance on the author of the universe and as we align our story to His.

Plodding wearily through each day, we realize that our strength is not our own—it belongs to One much bigger than us. In these dark caves of depression, we find light and hope to cling to when all else seems lost. Even when you don't understand why you have to walk this road, when you're hurting and dirt-smeared and broken, choose to embrace the story that He's given you as a way to understand Him better.

In our moments of weakness, on the days when we have to fight to simply get out of bed, we're given the gift of drawing closer to Him. For better or for worse, our faith will not emerge from this grief in the same state it entered. Use this time as an opportunity to cling to God. Arise from the ashes, battered and broken, but clutching the peace that surpasses understanding. Wherever you are in this journey with grief, lean in and embrace the lessons that God has in store for you. Ask Him to show you His redemptive work throughout your story. As your heart is squeezed tight in loss, allow it to help mould your life into something that is in constant reflection of God's glory. Let there be more to our grief than empty mourning; let there be Christ.

> *Not only that, but we rejoice in our sufferings, knowing that suffering produces endurance, and endurance produces character, and character produces hope, and hope does not put us to shame, because God's love has been poured into our hearts through the Holy Spirit who has been given to us.*
>
> —Romans 5:3–5

Journaling Prompts

Leaning into Grief, as You Lean on Christ

- What three words would you use to describe this loss? What three words would you use to describe what God has been teaching and showing you throughout it?

- What does it mean to you to find beauty within your story? Do you think it's possible?

- In what ways have you seen God redeem brokenness? Where do you see examples of hope within your story? What areas of this process do you still need to release to Him?

Chapter Sixteen

This Is Not the End

You may have made it to the end of this book, but we have certainly not arrived at the end of our journey. I hope that you land on this page with a journal full of tear-stained pages and hand-written messages of love. These words, poems, prayers, and letters are a gift to your sweet baby and to yourself. When we don't know how else to show the depth of our love, we allow ourselves to feel the depth of our grief.

I know that there are, however, days when we don't want to soak up knowledge from our misery. Sometimes the weight of this grief feels as if it is too much to carry—the lessons feel too difficult and raw. Growth involves aching bones and ugly stretch marks, emotional meltdowns and angry tantrums.

You and I both know just how messy and intricate, heartbreaking and frustrating, this thing called loss really is. Grief is never an easy task to undertake; it's difficult to grasp hold of something that is constantly changing and evolving. But if our exploration has pointed us back to the grace giving, all-knowing Author of our stories, then this waterlogged journal has been oh-so-worth-it. In our pain, let us never shy away from an opportunity to draw nearer to God.

While I was in the process of editing and reviewing this book, we miscarried again (twice, actually). The third miscarriage was our fourth loss and by far the most discouraging. The moment I first saw those burgundy stains, I knew that this was yet another chapter coming to a close. My heart ached along with the cramps in my abdomen, and my very being was bruised and wearied. I was so *done* with all this grief.

Trying to convince my toddler that we were on an adventure, I loaded up a backpack with tiny Thomas the Train toys and praised God that we were on a direct bus route to the hospital. Given that this wasn't my first miscarriage, I was painfully aware that there was nothing the doctors could do to stop the inevitable. While nurses entertained my son with Sesame Street stickers and bowlfuls of hospital Jell-O, I waited to be told that *it was over*. Poked and prodded by bloodwork technicians, I watched as little bits of my toddler's wobbly gelatin slid onto the emergency-room sheets, leaving orange stains. My mind grabbed hold of these mundane details; I needed to focus on something besides loss.

The doctors told us that we were experiencing a "threatened miscarriage" and that we had a 50/50 chance of losing the pregnancy. I left the hospital feeling sick and shaken. Tucking this baby tight to my heart, I held her close and tried to savour each and every moment. I knew we were losing her, but I fought hard to keep her. Although we were just less than eight weeks along, I shared a post on Facebook, telling the world about this precious little one and asking for prayer for strength, healing, and encouragement.

Incredibly, I awoke the next morning feeling as if I had been wrapped in a thick, woollen blanket of peace. The pain was significantly less than my previous two miscarriages, and I spent that weekend enveloped in the reassuring presence of God. With empty hands raised high, I let go of what little control I'd been trying to cling to and tried my best to simply trust.

That weekend brought answers to prayer—they just weren't the answers I'd been hoping for. Four days after the bleeding started, we lost the baby. This little one had only been given eight weeks with us, and although we didn't know the gender, we felt strongly that she was a girl. We said our good-bye and we named her Ebba, which means "strength."

But I didn't feel particularly strong. Quite the opposite, in fact. In my state of exhaustion, I felt as if someone had pushed me down a flight of stairs and then dragged me back up again, only to topple me over once more. Lying at the bottom of those stairs, covered in dishevelled bandages and new bumps, I didn't know how many times I could do this. Did I have the strength to try to climb again? What if I just kept falling, over and over, down further and further?

Reading my devotions later that evening, clinging to the psalms in the midst of my grief, I stumbled across Psalm 37:23–24: *"The steps of a man are established by the Lord, when he delights in his way; though he fall, he shall not be cast headlong, for the Lord upholds his hand."*

I wasn't climbing these stairs on my own, and it wasn't by chance that I'd ended up here. There is no biblical guarantee that we won't fall. There was no promise that these steps would be easy to climb, or that I wouldn't get bruised and bumped in the process, but there was the promise of a God who saves. I was falling, but there was a guardrail to grab onto. I would not be cast headlong. Cling to Him, and you won't be either.

You've begun recording your story, but this story isn't finished yet. This is but a small glimpse into God's great, eternity-bound book. We live in a world that is temporary. You and I are all too familiar with how quickly things pass away. We cannot keep our loved ones by holding them close; there's no promise that we (or our loved ones) will wake up tomorrow. But we can cling to the hope that this pain is momentary.

> *So we do not lose heart. Though our outer self is wasting away, our inner self is being renewed day by day. For this light momentary affliction is preparing for us an eternal weight of glory beyond all comparison, as we look not to the things that are seen but to the things that are unseen. For the things that are seen are transient, but the things that are unseen are eternal.*
> —2 Corinthians 4:16–18

As Christians, we don't need to fear difficult conversations or intimidating subjects. Death is not easy to think about. It's hard to embrace grief and confront the reality of our own mortality. But the value of our life is not measured by our time here on this earth. The choices we make in the here and now will define our attitude and perspective of life after death. We can choose to spend our days trembling and fearful, anxiously avoiding ambulance sirens and skydiving, or we can move forward with hope. We can cling to the knowledge that there is more to this life than what we see; we can say with assurance that we count it all *joy* that He considers us worthy of this present suffering for His name's sake. In Christ, we have hope of an eternal future. We know that we will never be more *alive* than when we stand before the throne of God, face to face, for eternity. We know that the funerals of our loved ones are not truly a good-bye but rather a "see you later."

For a short while, we've been parted from our babies. While we mourn that separation and long for a heavenly reunion, don't be afraid to truly *live*. In your pain and suffering, remember that *this* moment is an opportunity to glorify God. Glorifying God is not a prosperity gospel promise. We can choose to honour Him on both our best days and our worst; in our tears and in our pain, we have the chance to reflect Christ. In our weakness, we discover His strength.

As you continue to journal your way through grief, I pray that you will reach new heights. These past months or years have been hard. You've been sunk in the valleys and left fighting for footholds on a rocky path. Life isn't always a mountain-top experience, but you won't be *here* forever. There is an eternal perspective to your story. Your baby has moulded and shaped you, changed the way you view life, and been embedded upon your heart. It hurts to love deeply and to mourn authentically, but your little one's life was worth this pain. While you may not yet realize it, this sweet baby will continue to bring you to places you've never dreamed of. I know that it's not easy to stand where you're standing. This burden has been heavy and the road has been long, but your story is not yet finished. God is turning this tragedy into a triumph.

With gentle hands and a quiet voice, He transforms our grief into a testimony of His goodness. He shows us that the most beautiful way we can remember and celebrate our babies' lives is to simply glorify Him in the face of such loss. In Him, we find the strength to face tomorrow. In Him, our grief transforms into something beautiful.

He's given you this story. What are you going to do with it?

Acknowledgements

This isn't a book I wanted to write. It isn't a subject I wanted to be familiar with. But as I walked this road of loss, God began to peel back the layers of grief to reveal a journey that was infinitely sweeter and more joy-filled than I could have ever imagined. And so with a heart overflowing, I offer my thanksgivings to the God who comforts, heals, and redeems. In Him, life triumphs over death, and we find the freedom to share these stories with vulnerability and hope. All praise and glory be to God.

I also want to thank my family, especially my husband, who has shared this pain and has loved our babies so very well. Thank you for your encouragement to write, for your own openness to talk about loss, and for your lead-by-example faith. And to my kids, whose smiles get me through the difficult days and whose questions about life and death redirect my eyes heavenwards.

Thank you to my parents, for your constant love and unwavering support. For my mom, who passed away a few months before this book was published but never stopped praying or believing that this day would come.

Thank you to my friends and family. You have sent flowers and heart-filled texts, baked meals, and organized funeral flowers. You have entered into our grief and have mourned with us, remembering baby names and birth dates. All I can say is thank you. Each of you, in your own way, has helped to write this book. Your Christ-driven acts of love have been precious fuel to these pages.

And to the women who have shared their stories with me—you have filled this book with your heartache, your honesty, and your hope. It's an honour to include your words and your babies within these pages. These are the stories we need to hear more of. These stories hurt, but they also bind us together, allowing us to step into each other's pain as Christ first stepped into ours. Thank you for allowing me to share the bits of your story that are uncomfortable and messy in hopes of bringing light to this long-hidden topic.

Finally, thank you to my readers. I know your heart is aching, but I pray that you have found Christ on these pages. Thank you for your willingness to dig deeper and to come to the cross with arms open and palms up, ready to embrace.